Non-verbal Reasoning

11+ Handbook

Contents

Spatial awareness

Coded shapes and logic

Everyday practice

Introduction

What is an 11+ non-verbal reasoning exam?

Non-verbal reasoning is a test that focuses not on words or numbers, but on patterns, shapes and symbols. It is a common test for the 11+ as many people believe it to be an excellent means of determining a child's academic ability. Rather than being based on learning and recall, it tests whether a child is able to apply logic and reasoning.

The 11+ exam is taken when a child is at the end of Year 5 or in Year 6. It is a test used by state-funded grammar schools, selected academies and many of the independent schools. It is used to determine which children would most benefit from a more challenging academic education. Unlike most other exams, selective entrance tests usually cannot be retaken (although some schools do still set exams for entry at 12+ or 13+), so there is often fierce competition.

There are two main exam boards involved in producing non-verbal reasoning exams: GL Assessment and CEM (Durham University). GL Assessment uses a separate paper for non-verbal reasoning, while CEM tends to mix other 11+ subjects such as maths, English and verbal reasoning with non-verbal reasoning to create a paper divided into sections. There are other exam boards and individual schools who write their own papers and some schools will require children to complete the 11+ exam on a computer rather than on paper.

An 11+ non-verbal reasoning paper can be written in two formats, following either a multiple-choice or standard layout. For a multiple-choice paper, children will need to choose their answer from a set of options and mark it on a separate answer sheet. Answers must be marked in these booklets very carefully as the answer sheets are often read and marked by a computerised system. In the standard format, children must write each answer directly onto the question paper.

As with most exams, 11+ exam papers are timed, typically lasting between 45 minutes and one hour. The introduction of a timeframe can potentially have an impact on a child's performance, so it is important for children to work through practice materials in both timed and non-timed environments.

The scope and content of an 11+ non-verbal reasoning test can often differ across UK regions, as there is a range of question types that can be included. However, a paper will generally test a child's ability to:

- process graphic or pictorial information
- apply logical thinking and problem-solving skills
- understand how objects relate to each other in space (spatial awareness)
- find and follow patterns and rules
- apply maths skills such as rotation, reflection and symmetry
- work systematically.

These skills are tested through a series of questions that include the following types:

Identifying shapes

This is the ability to identify shapes that are similar or different and to sort shapes or symbols according to their features, such as shape, position, angle, number, size and shading.

Missing shapes

This is the ability to identify and apply a rule to find a missing shape. It includes the ability to see shapes within shapes and to make deductions from a given set of objects. Questions might include finding the most logical piece to fit into a grid, working out what comes next or deducing which larger shape a pattern has been taken from.

Rotating shapes

This is the ability to understand reflections and how shapes look in different orientations. Questions might include recognising mirror images or identifying matching nets and cubes.

Spatial awareness

This is the ability to visualise the result of changes to a shape. Questions might include determining the pattern made by holes punched in paper, matching 2D and 3D representations of shapes, or identifying rotations of shapes.

Coded shapes and logic

This is the ability to think logically and to make deductions about a set of symbols. Questions might include combining patterns together or assigning a code to a pattern element.

This book will help you to understand the key question types found in non-verbal reasoning exams. The Bond range of non-verbal reasoning assessment papers and the CEM maths and non-verbal reasoning books can be used alongside this book to apply the information. Bond also provide a range of exam test papers in both multiple-choice and standard format that will provide exam-style practice papers.

Identifying shapes

This group of question types tests your understanding and recognition of shape and pattern. It relies on:

- your ability to find shapes that are similar or different
- your skills for sorting given shapes or symbols according to their common features.

What types of features or links could objects or symbols have in common? You may need to consider any or all of the following elements:

A common link between shapes may not be immediately obvious. It may not always be a visible feature, so make sure you write down as many ideas as you can think of!

Exam tips

During an exam, jot down 'SPANSS' to remind you to check Shape, Position, Angle (direction), Number, Size and Shading. Use this system to quickly work through shapes that are alike, patterns that complete a pair, or work out which shape is the odd one out. Think of yourself like a computerised sorting machine working systematically through SPANSS.

There are three main sets of identifying shapes question types. These are:

- Recognise shapes that are similar and different
- Identify shapes and patterns
- Pair up shapes

You can work through this group of question types, looking at each set in turn.

1 *Recognise shapes that are similar and different*

The question types we will look at in this section are often referred to as similarities questions. They test your ability to work out which shapes are similar and which are different in a given set of options. You will need to use your observation skills to compare the given shapes and symbols and find the visual link or links.

REMEMBER!

It can be helpful to write down what the common feature isn't as well as what it might be!

Look at this example.

Which is the odd one out? Circle the letter.

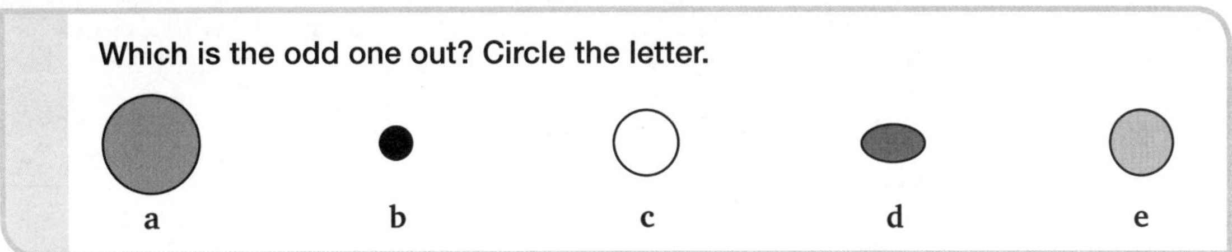

What immediately strikes you when you look at these options?

- They are all different sizes.
- They are all shaded differently.

So neither size nor shading can be the link here. Is there anything else about the shape of each option?

Starting from the left, look at each one in turn.

a is a circle **b** is a circle **c** is a circle **d** is an oval **e** is a circle

Four of the options are circles, so the odd one out must be d as it is a different shape.

Not all questions will use different-shaped options that can be seen quite quickly. Some links will be more subtle and you will need to look more closely to find the element they have in common.

Look at the next example.

Which is the odd one out? Circle the letter.

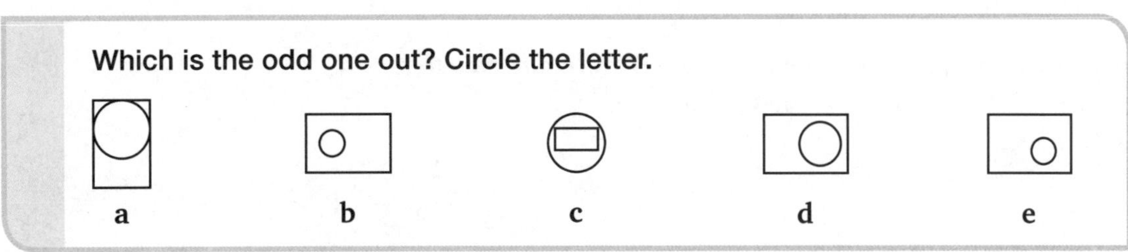

Unlike in the last example, each of these options is made up of the same shapes – a circle and a rectangle. Shape therefore cannot be the link here.

The circles and rectangles are different sizes in all of the symbols, so you cannot use size to find the answer.

Look at each option, starting with **a**. How would you describe each one?

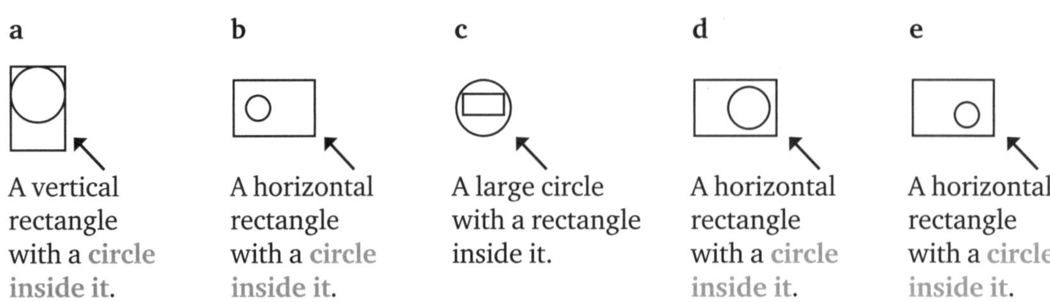

What do four of the shapes have in common? Shapes **a**, **b**, **d** and **e** are all made up of a rectangle with a circle inside. Option **c** shows the reverse. The positions of the circle and rectangle are different, so this option must be the odd one out.

You may need to use your knowledge of maths to answer some non-verbal reasoning questions. Here are two examples of where your maths skills would help you to find the answer to similarities questions.

REMEMBER!

To ensure you haven't missed any options, always work from left to right.

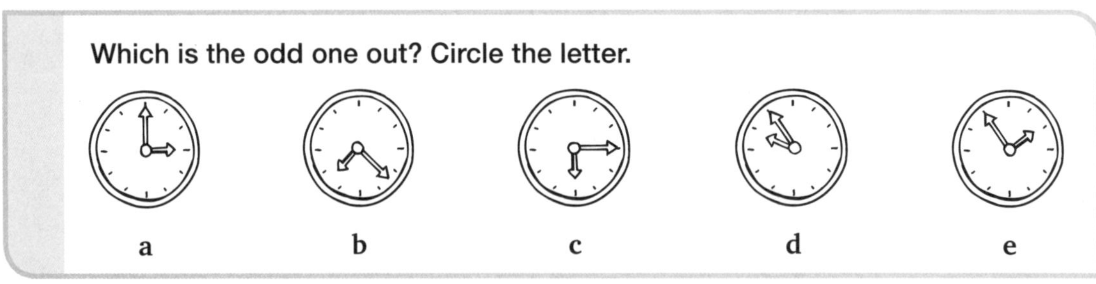

Each option shows the same circular clock face, so shape and size cannot be the link that will determine the answer. Look more closely at the symbols. What features make up each one?

Each symbol has:

- a small circle in the middle with two arrows connected to it
- 12 small lines that the arrows point towards
- two outer circles.

As they each have the same visible features, the link shared by four of the symbols must be something more subtle.

Although each option is made up of the same elements, they do all look different. Why? The clock faces are showing different times, so the two arrows are in different positions in each shape. Look at each option in turn and describe what you can see.

a The time is three o'clock.
The position of the arrows **makes a right angle** (90°).

b The time is about 23 minutes past seven.
The position of the arrows **makes a right angle** (90°).

c The time is quarter past six.
The position of the arrows **makes a right angle** (90°).

d The time is five minutes to ten.
The arrows are much closer together. They do not make a right angle in this position.

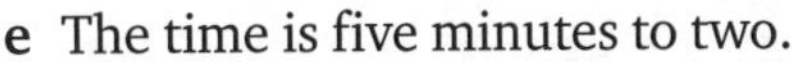

e The time is five minutes to two.
The position of the arrows **makes a right angle** (90°).

Looking closely at each of the options shows us that the arrows make right angles in **a**, **b**, **c** and **e**. You need to draw on your knowledge of **angles** in order to work out that the odd one out in this question is **d**.

Now look at this example.

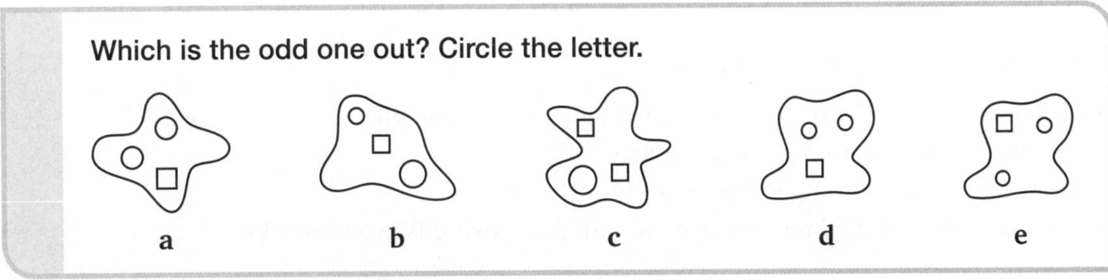

You can see quite quickly that:

- the outline of each shape is different
- each one contains circles and squares
- the position of the circles and squares is different in each option.

None of these elements will lead you to the answer.

So, starting with **a**, think about how you could describe each shape. It may help to draw a grid to note down what you can see.

Shape	Number of circles	Number of squares
a	2	1
b	2	1
c	1	2
d	2	1
e	2	1

It is clear from the information in the grid that the odd one out is c; it has one less circle and one more square than the other four shapes. The link here relates to **number**.

These last two examples of similarities question types test your observation skills rather than your knowledge of maths.

Look at the first example.

Which is the odd one out? Circle the letter.

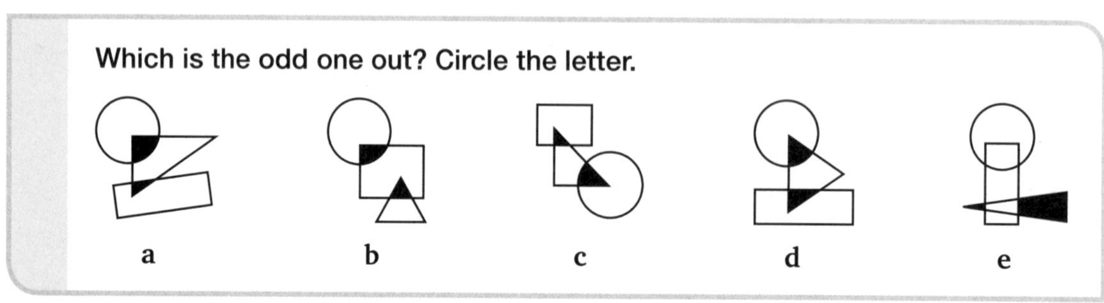

A quick look at each option shows that:

- each symbol is made up of a circle, a triangle and a rectangle
- the circle in each option is the same size
- the triangles and rectangles are all different sizes
- the circle, triangle and rectangle are in different positions in each option.

Shape, size and position can therefore be eliminated, as none of these elements can be the common feature between four of the symbols.

Look again at the symbols. How are the individual shapes connected in each one?

a

The area where the circle and triangle overlap is shaded.

The area where the triangle and rectangle overlap is shaded.

b

The area where the circle and rectangle overlap is shaded.

The area where the rectangle and triangle overlap is shaded.

c

The area where the rectangle and triangle overlap is shaded.

The area where the triangle and circle overlap is shaded.

d

The area where the circle and triangle overlap is shaded.

The area where the triangle and rectangle overlap is shaded.

e

The area where the circle and rectangle overlap is not shaded.

The area where the rectangle and triangle overlap is not shaded.

The parts of the triangle that do not overlap with the rectangle are shaded.

By breaking each symbol down and looking at the individual shapes that make up each one, it is easier to see how each symbol is put together. Using this method, you can clearly see that the odd one out is e, as the other four symbols have shaded areas where the shapes overlap.

Here is the second example.

Which is the odd one out? Circle the letter.

a **b** **c** **d** **e**

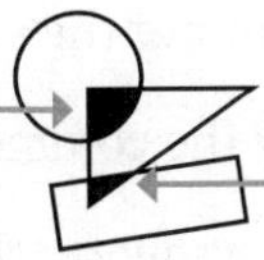

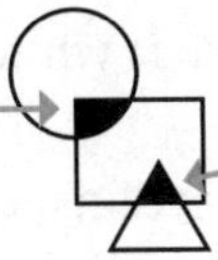

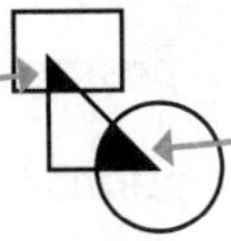

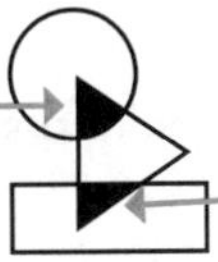

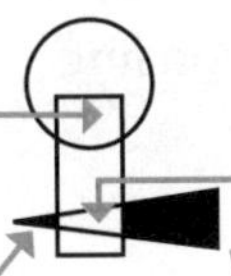

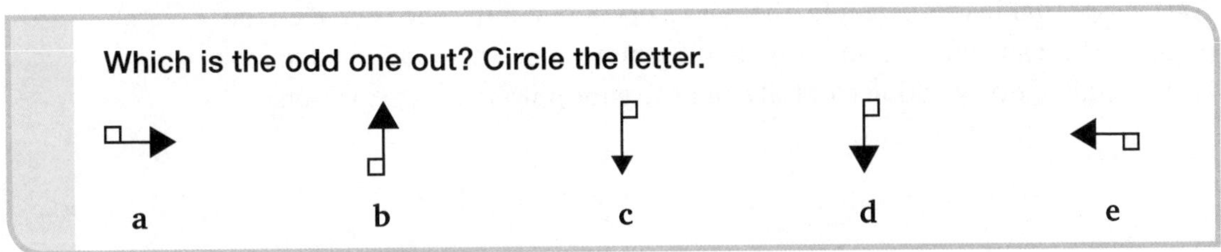

Looking at these symbols quickly they all seem very similar. This means the feature that makes one stand out as being 'odd' compared to the other four options must be a very slight change. You must look at each option very carefully to find the common feature that four of the symbols share.

Can you eliminate any elements from being the common link?

- Each symbol is made up of an arrow and a square; the link cannot be to do with shape.
- Each arrow is shaded black and each square is white; the link cannot be to do with shading.
- The arrows are all pointing in different directions; the link cannot be to do with direction.
- The square is on the left-hand side of some arrows and on the right-hand side of others; the link cannot be to do with position.

What else could be different for one of these options?

Working from left to right, break each symbol down and look at the two shapes individually.

1 The square in option **a** is the same size as the squares in **b**, **c**, **d** and **e**. This cannot be used to identify the odd one out.

2 The arrow in option **a** is the same length as the arrows in each of the other symbols. This will not lead us to the common link.

3 The arrowhead in option **a** is:

- the **same size** as the arrowhead in **b**
- larger than the arrowhead in **c**
- the **same size** as the arrowhead in **d**
- the **same size** as the arrowhead in **e**.

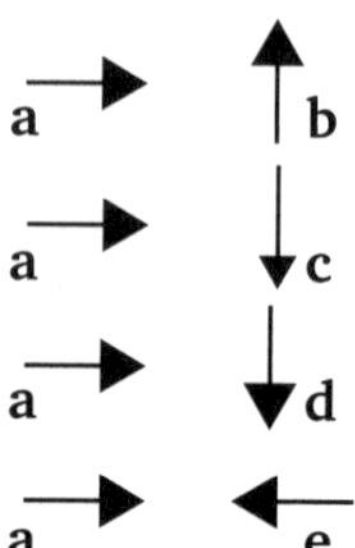

Has a common feature been found that is shared by four of the options? Yes, the arrowheads in **a**, **b**, **d** and **e** are all the same size. Symbol c has a smaller arrowhead, so this must be the odd one out.

You can see that in this example, there is a very subtle difference between the options. This can make questions more difficult to answer, so you need to look at the detail of every option carefully and use your powers of observation.

2 *Identify shapes and patterns*

This set also contains a similarities question type, so your observation skills and understanding of visual connections between shapes and patterns are being tested here too.

However, this type is presented in a different format from the similarities questions we have already looked at. This time you must work out the common link within a group of given shapes and then identify the option that also shares that common link or feature.

We know now that symbols can share a range of possible features. Look at this example. It shows how a variety of common links may be combined.

REMEMBER!

Make sure you find all the connections in the given set – you need to find the option that shares all of these links.

Which pattern on the right belongs in the group on the left? Circle the letter.

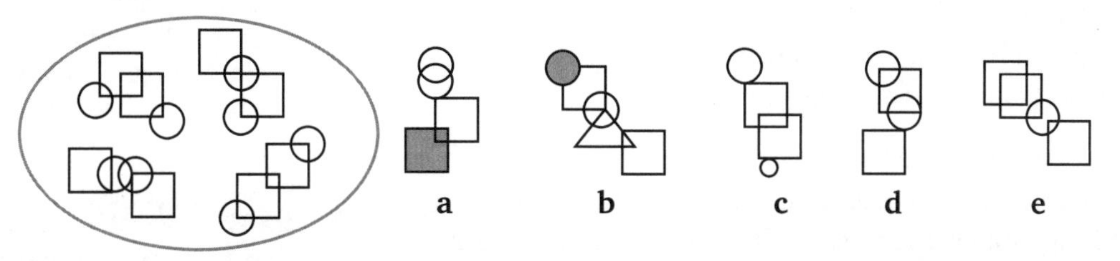

Often, symbols can share more than one common link or feature. Look closely at the symbols in the given set in turn. What do you notice about each one?

1 Each symbol is made up of only two squares and two circles.
2 The squares and circles are the same size for all symbols.
3 The squares and circles are in different positions in each symbol.
4 None of the shapes are shaded.

Think about the conclusions you can draw from your observations, and as you go through them you may be able to cross out some of the answer options.

- Must have only two squares and two circles. So NOT **b** or **e**
- Squares and circles must be the same size as in the given set. So NOT **c**
- Squares and circles can be in any position.
- Shapes will have no shading. So NOT **a** or **b**

With options **a**, **b**, **c** and **e** eliminated, option **d** is identified as the answer.

In some questions the shapes given at the beginning may seem very different, but, as before, look carefully to find what they have in common.

For example:

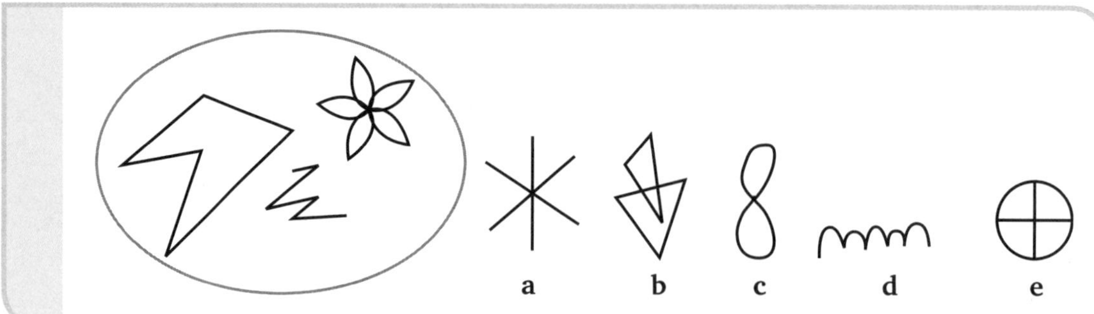

The first three patterns look very different.

- No shape, size or shading in common.
- No position or angle features in common.
- No combination of line styles in common.
- No number of lines or angles in common.
- But all have five elements in them.

So working through the answer options, **a** has six lines, **b** has two triangles and so six lines, **c** has two sections, **d** has five curves and **e** has four sections, so the best fit is d with five parts.

REMEMBER!

Remember, symbols can be connected by a combination of any of these elements: size, position, angles, number, shape or shading.

REMEMBER!

Cross out an option as soon as you have discounted it. This will help you to clearly see what's left.

3 *Pair up shapes*

The question types that make up this set are called analogies. You may be familiar with this type of question from verbal reasoning tests. In both verbal and non-verbal reasoning, analogy questions test your ability to spot a connection between two concepts. You must then be able to apply this same relationship to something else.

The difference with the non-verbal reasoning type is that these questions involve visual analogies – you must identify the link between a pair of given pictures, shapes or patterns rather than words.

You will usually be given one pair of images that are connected in a particular way and the first image of a second pair. You have to find the correct image to complete the second pair in the same way as the first pair.

As with the similarities group, analogies can be based on a variety of different connections. Don't worry if you can't see a link straight away. You will find that some links will be easier to see than others.

We'll start with some of the more straightforward examples.

Which shape or pattern completes the second pair in the same way as the first pair?

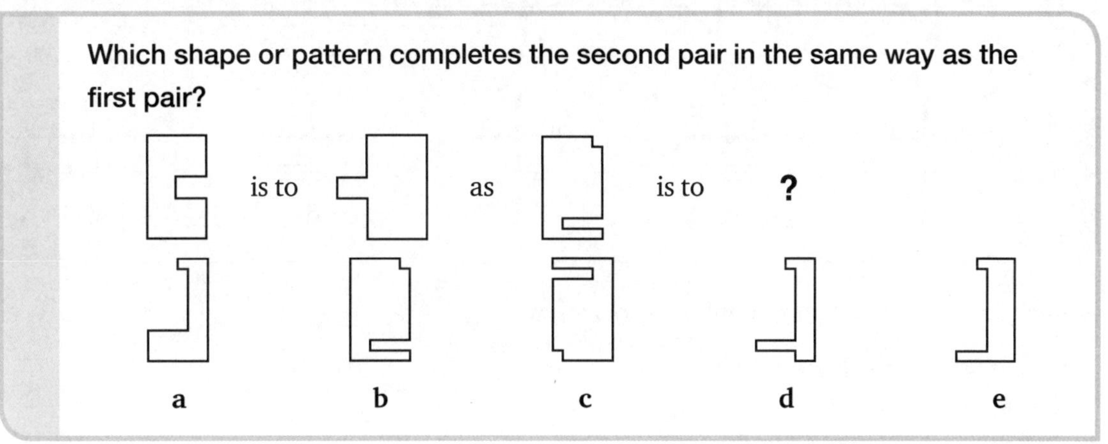

1 Look carefully at the first pair of shapes. How would you describe them?

The first shape is a rectangle with a small piece missing from the centre.

The second shape is a rectangle with a small additional piece jutting out in the centre.

2 How might these two shapes be connected?

If both shapes were joined together, the second symbol would complete the first one to form one whole rectangle.

3 Now you have found the visual link that connects the first pair, apply this to the second pair.

Which option will make a complete rectangle when joined with the first shape of the second pair?

4 Following this careful checking process you will find that option d will make a complete rectangle when joined with the given shape.

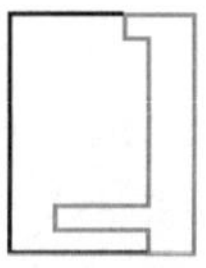

This first example shows how analogies can be based on shape. Now look at an example with a different type of connection.

Which shape or pattern completes the second pair in the same way as the first pair? Circle the letter.

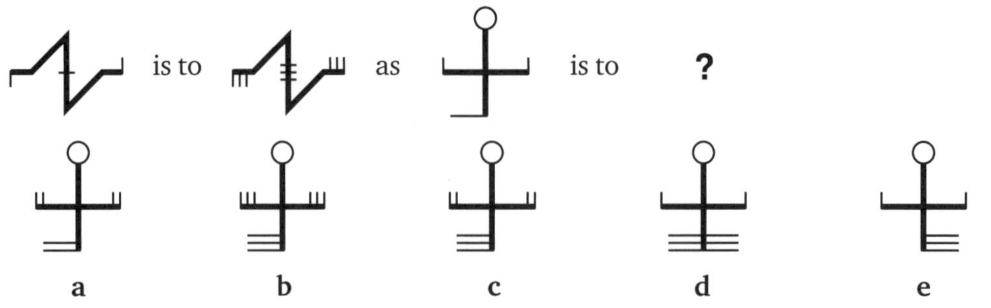

A quick look at the first pair of objects shows that:

- they are the same shape
- they are the same size
- they are in the same position
- the thickness of the lines is the same.

None of these elements can form the link between the objects. So what differences can you see between the two shapes?

The connection between these two shapes is related to number; each short single line in the first symbol has become three short lines in the second symbol.

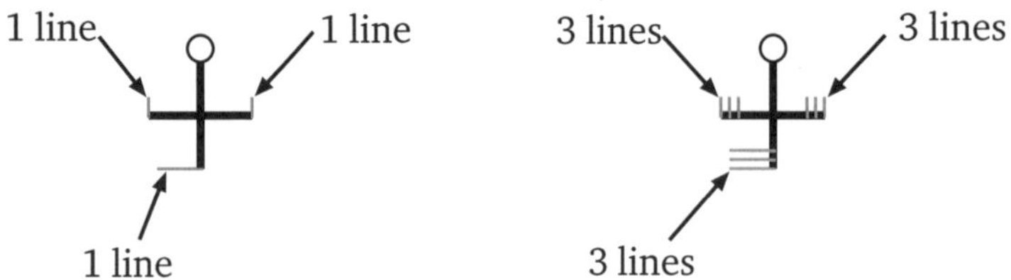

Now you can use this analogy to predict which symbol will complete the second pair.

This predicted symbol matches option **b**, so this must be the answer.

This next version of an analogy question also uses a connection that can be quite simple to identify.

Which shape or pattern completes the second pair in the same way as the first pair? Circle the letter.

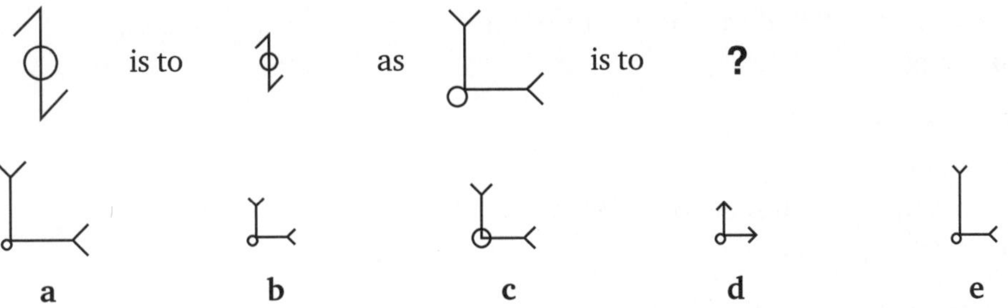

What do you notice about the first pair?

- They are the same shape.
- They are in the same position.

So, how would you describe the connection between the two shapes?

The second image is a smaller copy of the first one; the connection between these shapes relates to **size**. There is no other change, so this rule can be applied easily to the second pair.

Work through each option and compare them with the given shape to find the answer. As before, it can be helpful to make brief notes about each option in a grid.

> **REMEMBER!**
> Check all options carefully to make sure you find the best answer.

Looking carefully at the options in this example, you should find that the correct answer is **b**:

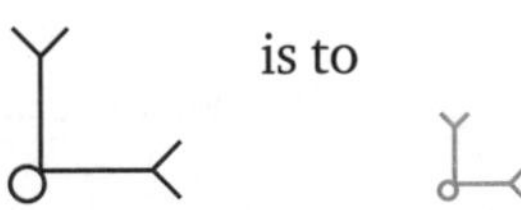

This next example shows another common link that is often used in visual analogy questions.

Which shape or pattern completes the second pair in the same way as the first pair? Circle the letter.

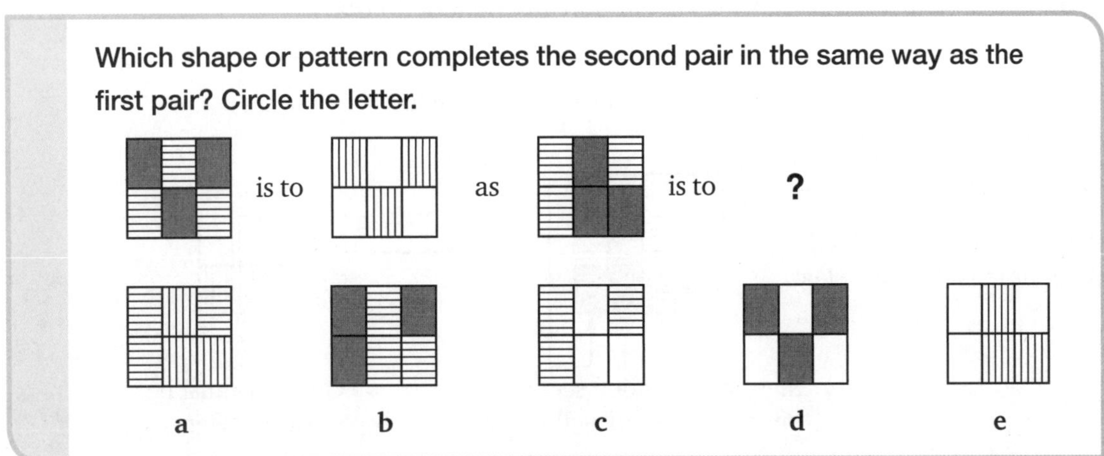

You should be able to see quite quickly that the connection for this analogy question relates to **shading**.

Before you look at exactly how the shading is different, though, make sure that there are no other differences between the first pair. In this example, the objects are:

- the same shape
- the same size
- split into the same number of sections
- in the same position.

So, look more closely at the shading. How does the shading in the first shape change in the second shape?

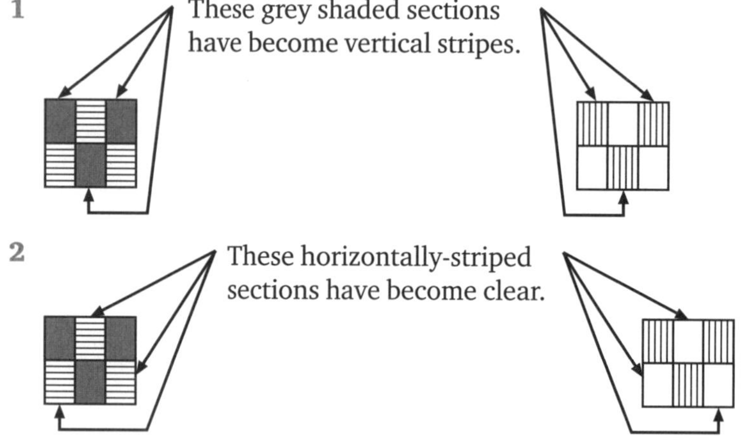

Now look at the first shape in the second pair. How will the shape change when these rules are applied?

You know that the correct option must have a combination of clear sections and striped sections. You can therefore discount options **a**, **b** and **d** straight away.

Compare options **c** and **e** with the given shape. Which one has the shading in the correct position?

We know that:

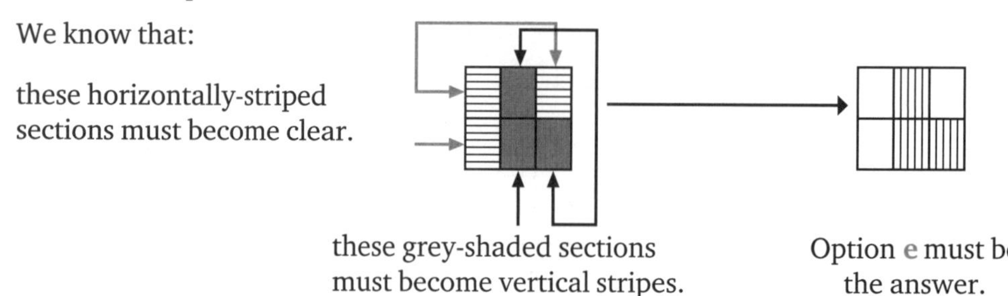

There are several variations of visual analogy questions that are based around links with **position**. For some of these questions you will need to rely on your basic understanding of certain key maths topics, such as: angles, symmetry, reflection and rotation.

Look at these examples.

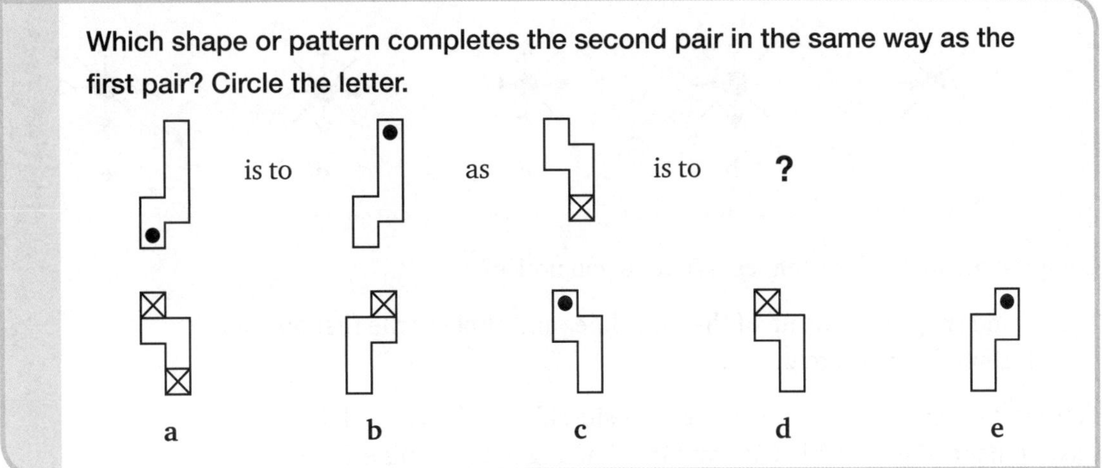

What do you notice about the first pair? Can you see the connection between the two shapes?

The shapes are identical except for the position of the shaded circle. It has moved from the bottom of the shape to the top.

This connection can now be applied to the second pair.

Remember to look closely at all the options. In this example, options **b** and **d** are very similar. The correct option must be **d** as it is the same shape as the given symbol.

The next two examples show more complex position changes. These may seem confusing at first but if you break the images down and look at them in sections it is easier to see what is going on.

Which shape or pattern completes the second pair in the same way as the first pair? Circle the letter.

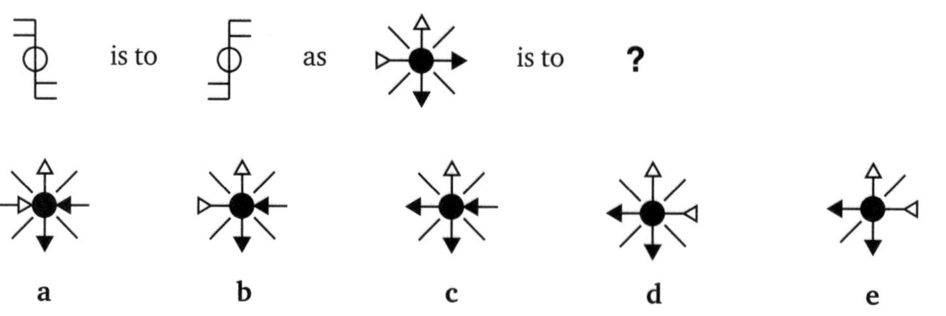

Compare the first pair of shapes. What do you notice?

The second shape is made up of the same lines and circle as the first one but there is something different.

The short horizontal lines are on the opposite sides of the vertical line in the second shape. Can you think of anything that might cause this effect?

Imagine that a mirror has been placed on the dotted line shown on the right. What would the mirror image of the shape look like?

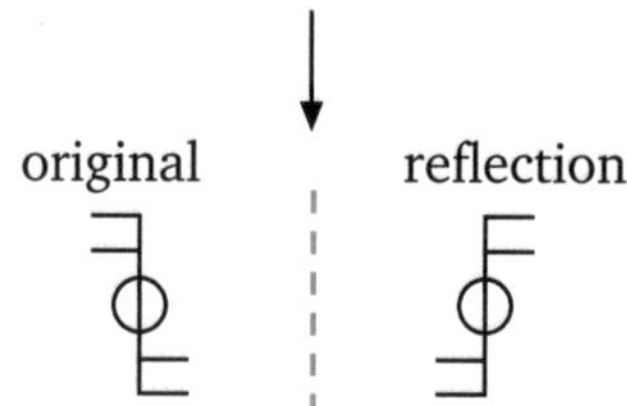

The link between the first pair relates to reflection; the second shape is the mirror image or reflection of the first shape.

This rule can now be applied to the second pair.

In this example, the first shape of the second pair has several elements, so it may appear more difficult to work out.

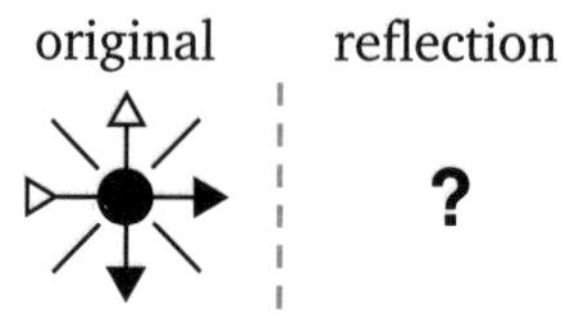

For complex shapes like this, try to look at each section individually and think about how each one would be reflected in a mirror. This will help you to build up a full picture of the answer.

Here, you might start by thinking about the vertical arrows and the circle in the middle. What would they look like in a mirror?

The reflection of these shapes would look the same.

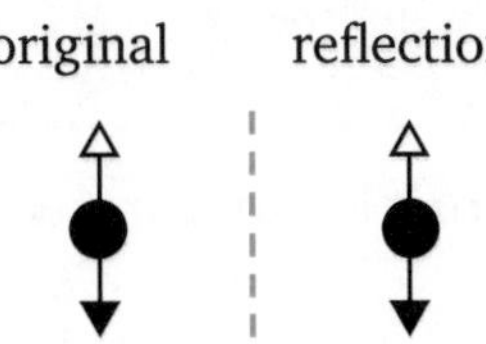

Next, you could look at the diagonal lines.

What would these look like?

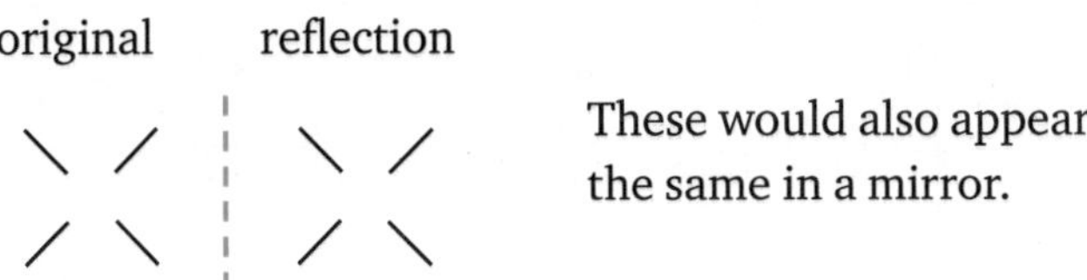

These would also appear the same in a mirror.

You could then think about the horizontal arrows one at a time.

Would the reflection of the black arrow look different to the original?

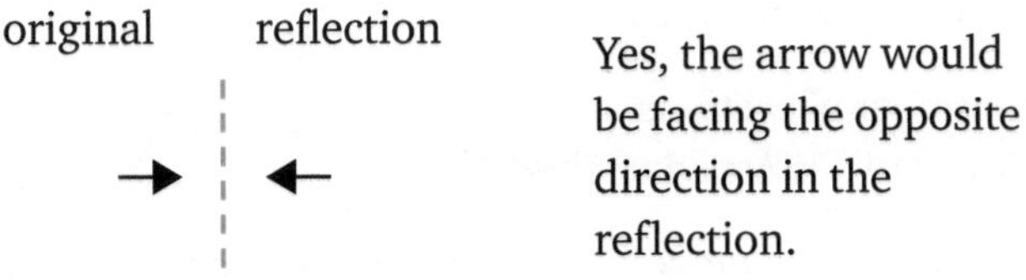

Yes, the arrow would be facing the opposite direction in the reflection.

Lastly, think about the white-headed arrow.

Would this change?

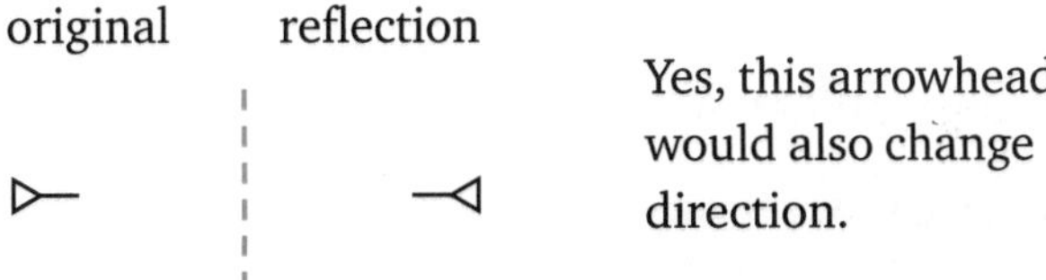

Yes, this arrowhead would also change direction.

Now that you have thought about how each part of the symbol would look in a mirror, you need to put all of the elements together to find the answer.

> **REMEMBER!**
>
> It can be helpful to draw a quick sketch of what you think the reflected shape will look like. You can then compare this with the options given.

Looking carefully at the options in this example, you should find that the correct answer is **d**:

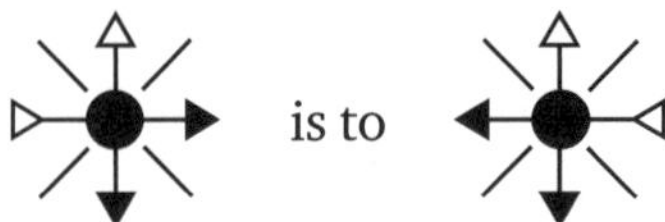

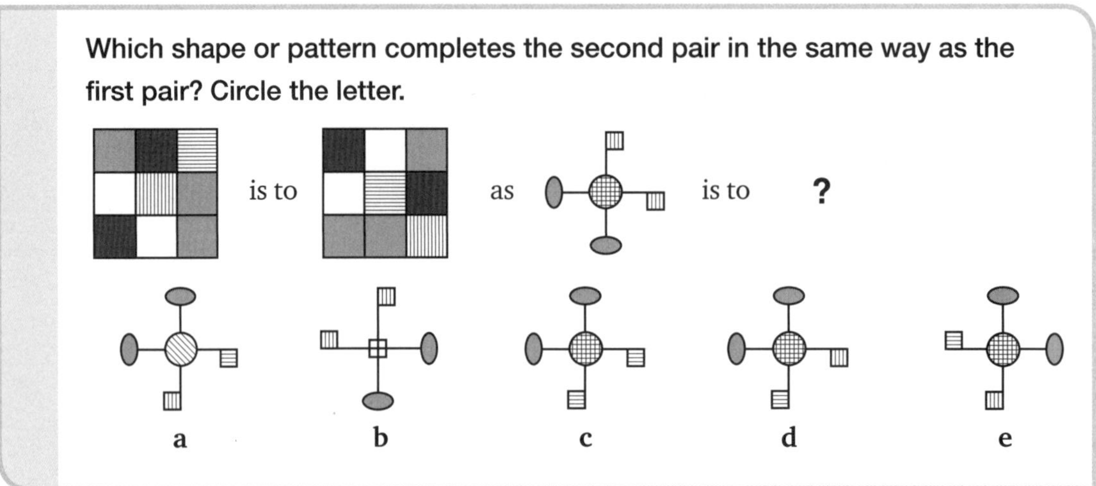

Look at another example that may seem difficult to work out at first glance.

A quick look at the first pair of shapes shows that:

- they each have the same number of sections
- the same number of sections are patterned or shaded.

It is clear, though, that the shading has changed. Unlike in the example on page 18, the sections which have the same type of shading have not all been replaced with another type of shading. For example, the darker shaded section in the middle of the top row becomes white in the second shape, but the darker shaded section in the bottom left corner becomes light grey in the second shape, not white.

So what has made the shading appear different?

What would the first shape look like if you turned it?

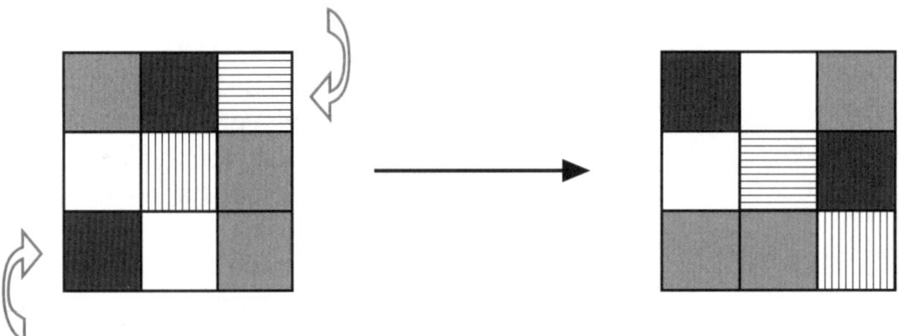

The position of the first shape has been changed; it has been rotated 90 degrees clockwise to form the second shape.

This rotation link can now be applied to complete the second pair.

What would this shape look like if it was rotated 90 degrees clockwise?

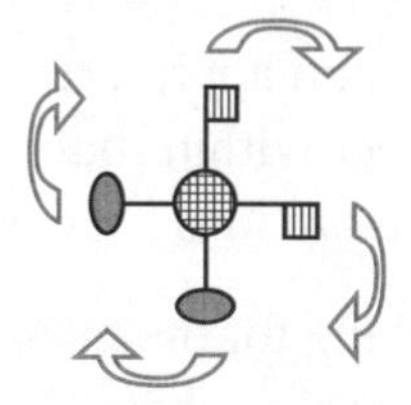

Take one element at a time and think about what its new position would be once the shape is rotated.

Next, think about whether any of the shading will be affected by the rotation.

You may find it helpful to make brief notes so you can discount incorrect options quickly. As soon as you can discount an option, move on to the next one.

Making notes in a grid about the correct option criteria can be useful.

REMEMBER!

Notice what happens to vertically and horizontally striped shading when it is rotated.

Option	Same shape?	Correct positions?	Correct shading?
a	✓	✓	✗ – shading in circle shown as diagonal lines
b	✗ – should be a circle in the middle	—	—
c	✓	✓	✓
d	✓	✓	✗ – line shading in right-hand square is the wrong direction
e	✓	✗ – one grey oval in the wrong position	—

From these notes we can deduce that the correct option in this example must be c.

REMEMBER!

Drawing a quick sketch can often help you to visualise a rotated shape. If you find this hard, try turning the paper round in the direction the shape needs to move.

Missing shapes

This group of question types also tests your understanding of shape and pattern. It relies on your ability to:

- identify and apply a rule
- see shapes within shapes and patterns within patterns
- make deductions from given sets of objects or symbols.

When looking for the missing part of a larger pattern, what type of features should you think about? Look again at the spider diagram from the first section, Identifying shapes:

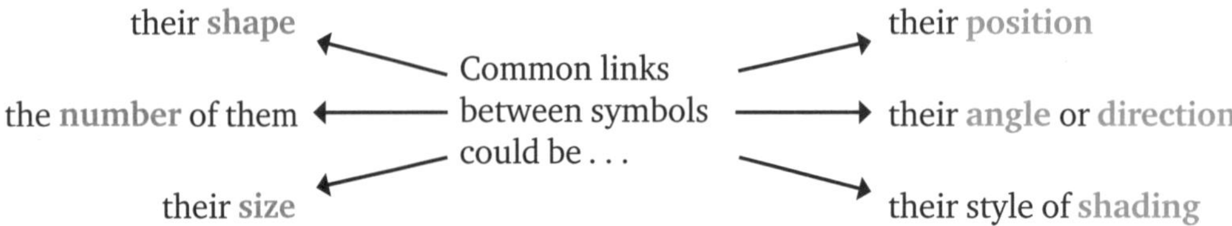

As well as using these features to find common links and similarities, these elements can also help you to identify a missing shape or symbol. For example, a series or pattern of symbols may be based on:

- an increase or decrease in size or number
- alterations in shape, shading, position or direction.

There are three main sets of missing shapes questions. These are:

- Find shapes that complete a sequence
- Find a given part within a shape
- Find a missing shape from a pattern

REMEMBER!

A pattern or sequence may involve more than one element and different rules may have been applied to different features. Always look carefully and note down as many features as you can so that no aspect is overlooked or forgotten.

Exam tips

Don't waste precious time in exams staring at the whole shape. Instead, immediately look at the different sections and how the patterns are changing, then find the missing option. If you do struggle with a question, try to reduce your options by rejecting as many as possible. Ultimately, take the best guess and move on. You can always come back to any tricky questions if you have time.

Now we'll work through this group of question types, looking at each one in turn.

4 Find shapes that complete a sequence

The question types we will look at in this section are often referred to as **sequences** questions. They test your ability to identify and apply a given rule or rules in order to find the missing step in a sequence of images. You will need your observation and analysis skills to solve these question types.

Look at some examples, starting with one of the more straightforward sequences you may come across in a test paper.

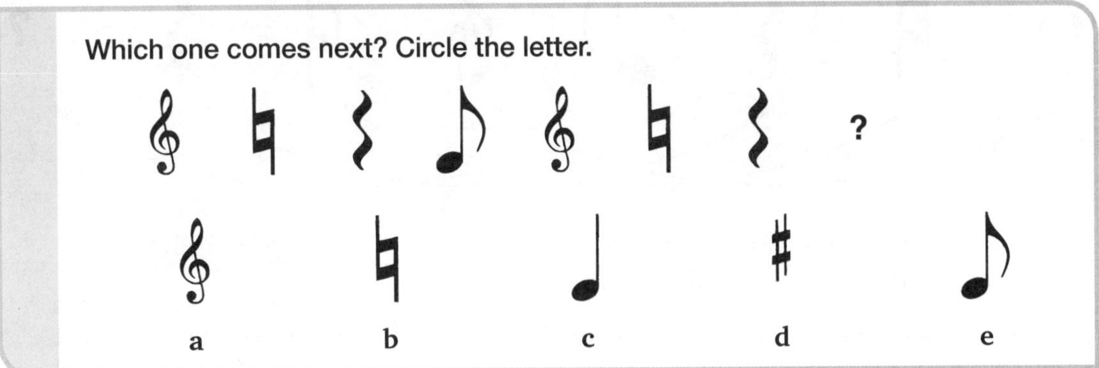

You need to find the next shape in the line and as this is a sequence question, you know that the missing symbol will be connected in some way to the symbols that are before it. What do you immediately notice about this row of symbols?

- They are all connected with music.
- They are all shaded black.
- They all appear upright and are similar in size.

So the type, shading, position and size of these symbols will not give any clues for working out the rule applied to this sequence.

Think about the first symbol (the treble clef) and look along the line. What do you notice? The treble clef reappears as the fifth symbol.

Now look at the second symbol (the 'natural sign'). As you look along the line you will see that this also reappears as the sixth symbol.

The symbols are being repeated; this is a **repeating pattern**. Now that the rule has been identified, it can easily be applied to find the symbol that comes next.

You know that the treble clef is the first and the fifth symbol. The treble clef must therefore start the repeating block. If it helps you to focus on the symbols, underline the repeating block.

Now match the pairs of symbols. Drawing arrows to link the pairs can help you see which symbol should come next.

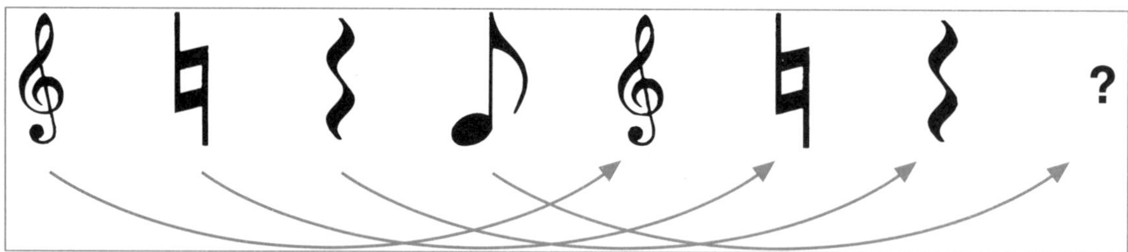

Finally, look through the options and select the correct answer. In this example, the missing symbol is option e, the quaver.

This method can be used to solve any repeating sequence question, whether the sequence of images is made up of pictures, symbols, shapes or other patterns. Some answer options may be very similar, such as option **c** (the crotchet) and option **e** (the quaver) in this example. To make sure you choose the right answer, check all the options very carefully.

In this first example the missing part of the sequence was at the end of the line of symbols. Not all sequence questions will follow this format. Here is an example where the missing link is within the sequence rather than at the end. You need to pay close attention to detail in this style of question.

> **REMEMBER!**
>
> Repeating sequences are one of the easiest and quickest types of sequence questions to solve. Check for a repeating block first, before looking for any other rules and patterns in sequence questions.

Which one completes the sequence? Circle the letter.

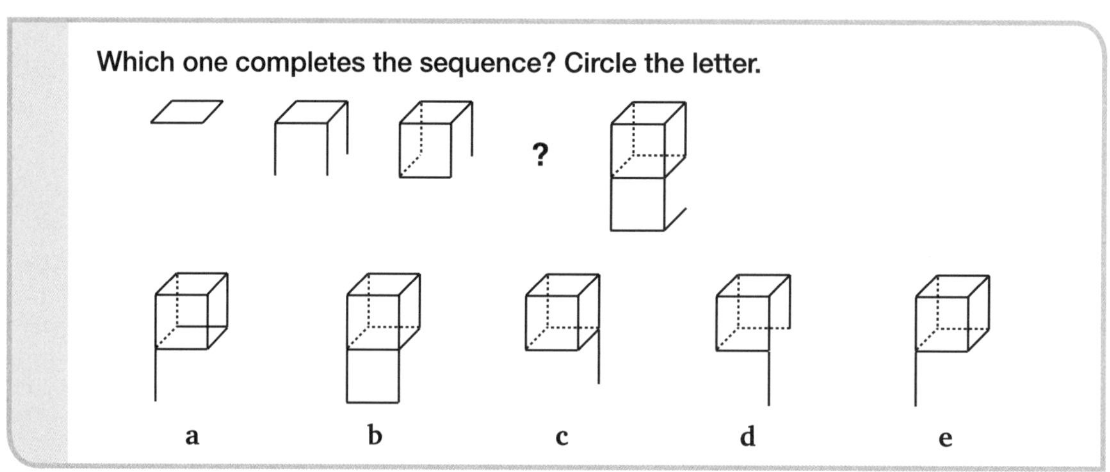

You should be able to see quite quickly that this is not a repeating sequence. How would you describe what you can see?

- The steps in the sequence seem to be building a 3D shape.
- The shape grows larger at each stage.
- Some lines are dashed and some lines are solid.

How does the symbol change at each stage? Look at the first two steps. How is the shape different in the second step from the first step?

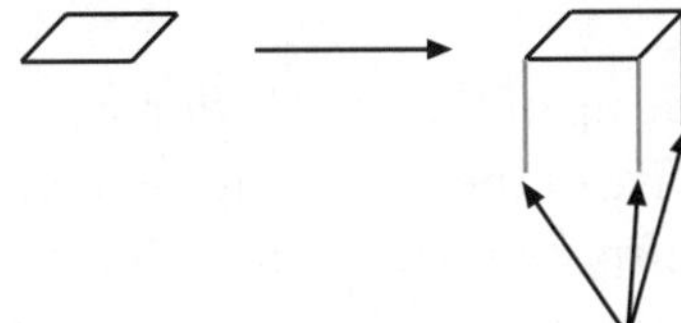

3 lines have been added

Now compare the second and third steps. How has the shape changed at the third step?

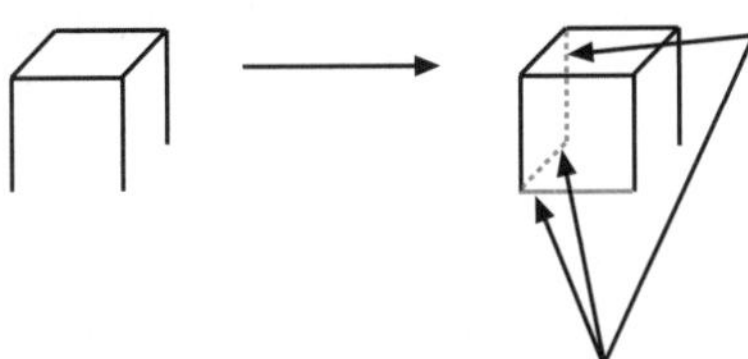

3 lines have been added

Has a common rule been found for the first three steps of this sequence? Yes, three lines have been added at each step in the sequence.

The fourth step in the sequence is the missing link you need to find but you know now that it must be made up of the third step plus three more lines. However, before you can work out which of the options is correct you must look at the final image of the sequence.

How is the fifth step different from the third step in the sequence?

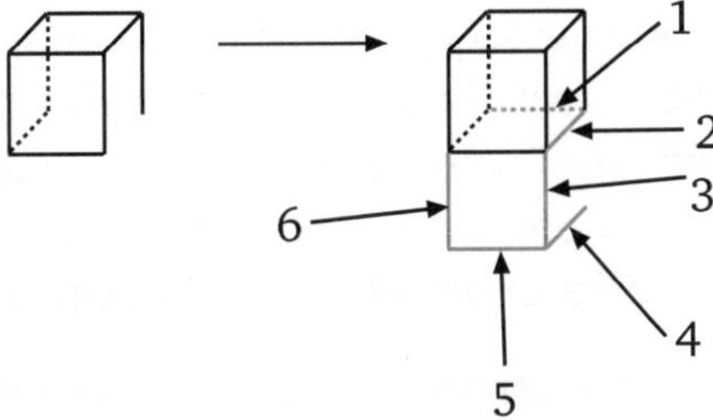

6 lines have been added

You have identified the additional lines that make up the final step in the sequence. Now you can look for the option that is made up of the third step, plus three of the lines that the fifth step contains.

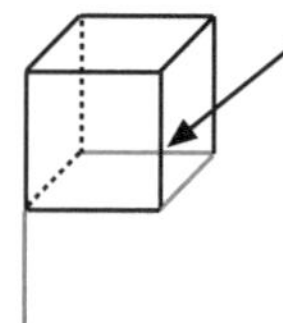

Option **a** is made up of the third step plus three of the lines from the fifth step. But are the lines exactly the same? No. Look at the line the arrow is pointing to. In the fifth step this is a dashed line, not a solid one. This cannot be the missing step.

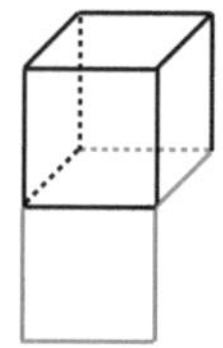

Option **b** is made up of the third step plus five of the lines from the fifth step. This does not follow the rule so cannot be the missing step.

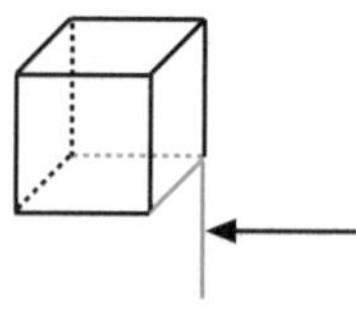

Option **c** is made up of the third step plus three more lines. But are all of these lines present in the fifth step? No. Look at the line the arrow is pointing to. This is not drawn in the fifth step of the sequence. This cannot be the missing step.

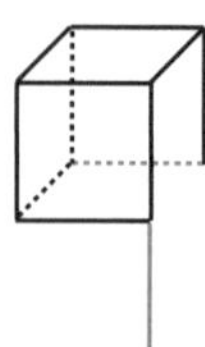

Option **d** is made up of the third step but it only has two of the lines from the fifth step. This cannot be the missing step.

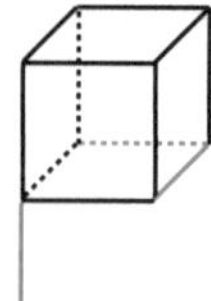

Option **e** is made up of the third step plus three of the lines from the fifth step. **This is the missing step.**

It can be quite difficult to find the right option in sequences where the missing step is not at the end of the sequence. If you break the sequence down into steps and compare each step with the next one, it will make it easier to find the rule. Following a methodical and careful approach like the one shown here will ensure you find the missing symbol, wherever it is placed in the sequence.

The last example showed how changes to **shape** can form the link in a sequence. The next example looks at another common linking feature which requires your observation skills.

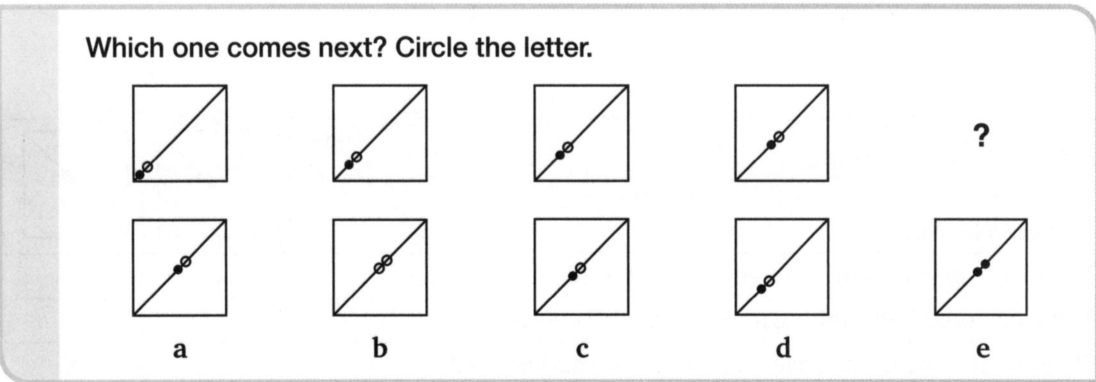

What are the first points that come to mind when you look at this sequence of images?

Each picture is the same size and is made up of:

- a square
- a diagonal line pointing in the same direction
- one clear circle and one circle shaded black.

None of these elements will help you to find the image that comes next. What else can you see?

- Both of the circles are on the diagonal line.
- The clear circle is always above the black circle.
- The position of the circles changes in each step.

This last observation highlights a difference from one step of the sequence to the next. How does the position of the pair of circles change?

As the sequence progresses, the two circles move together along the diagonal line towards the top right-hand corner of the square. You can now use this rule to work out which image should come next.

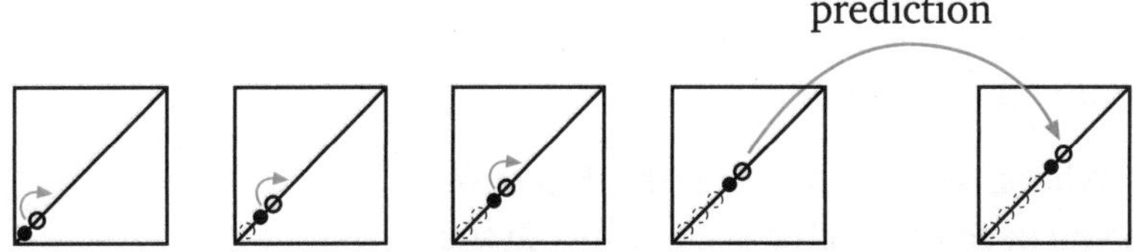

The circles were halfway along the line in the last given step. They will therefore need to be above the halfway position in the final step of this sequence.

First, use this rule to eliminate any options where the circles are not above the halfway point. This will make it faster to identify the answer. Following this process leaves options **a** and **b**.

Now compare these options with the common features you noted when you first looked at the sequence. You might find it helpful to use a grid for this.

Common feature \ Option		
Is it made up of a square, diagonal line and 2 circles?	✓	✓
Is the diagonal line running in the same direction?	✓	✓
Does it have one clear circle and one circle shaded black?	✓	✗

You can stop the comparison here; option **b** has two clear circles so cannot be the missing step. Option a must be the correct answer.

This next example shows how you can use your maths knowledge to help work out the connection and rule for some sequence questions.

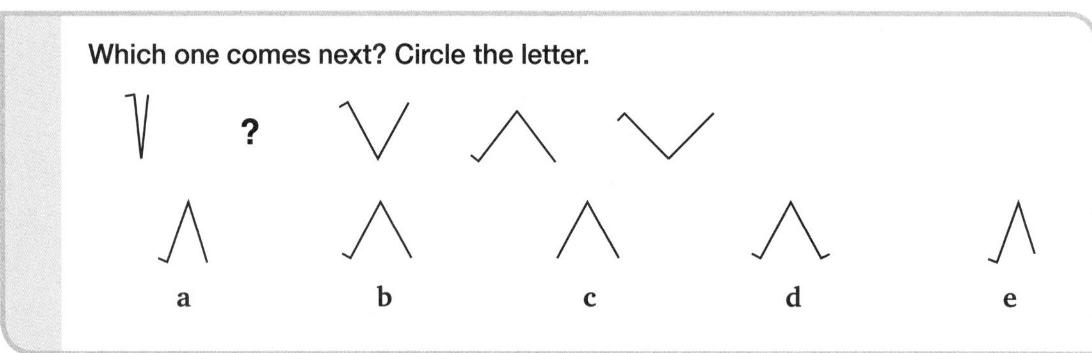

First, think about the features that each of the symbols share:

- They are all V-shaped.
- They are all made up of three lines; one short line and two longer lines.
- The short lines are all the same length.
- The longer pairs of lines are all the same length.
- The short line is always in front of the longer lines.

Now look at the symbols again. What makes each step of the sequence different from the next one? As you need to find the second step in this sequence, it is easier to look at the changes that occur between the last three consecutive symbols first.

1 The angle between the two longer lines increases with each step.

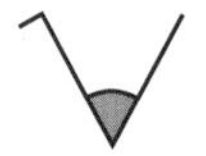  

2 The **direction** of the V-shape alternates, pointing down then up.

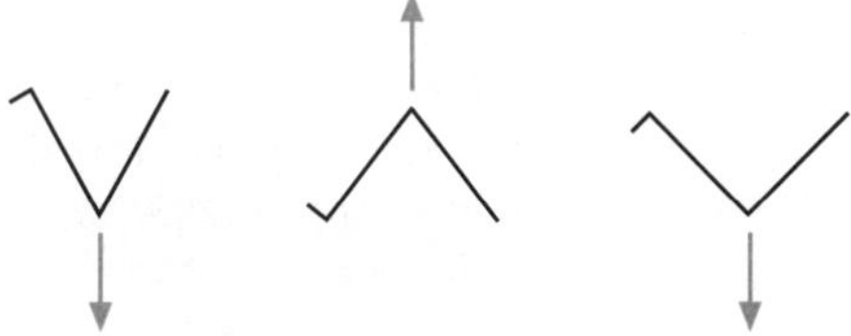

3 The **direction** of the short line alternates, pointing down then up.

Keeping these differences in mind, you can now draw some conclusions about the missing symbol:

- It must have an angle greater than the first step and less than the third step.
- The direction of the V-shape must point upwards.
- The direction of the short line must point upwards.

You can now combine the checklist of common features with these conclusions and compare them with each option to identify the answer. As before, it can be helpful to make notes in a grid.

Following this process, you will find that option **a** is the correct answer to this example.

So far we have looked at how rules relating to repetition, shape, position, angle and direction can all form the basis of a sequence. This next example shows a simple version of another common feature that can be used in many different ways to create sequence questions.

Which one comes next? Circle the letter.

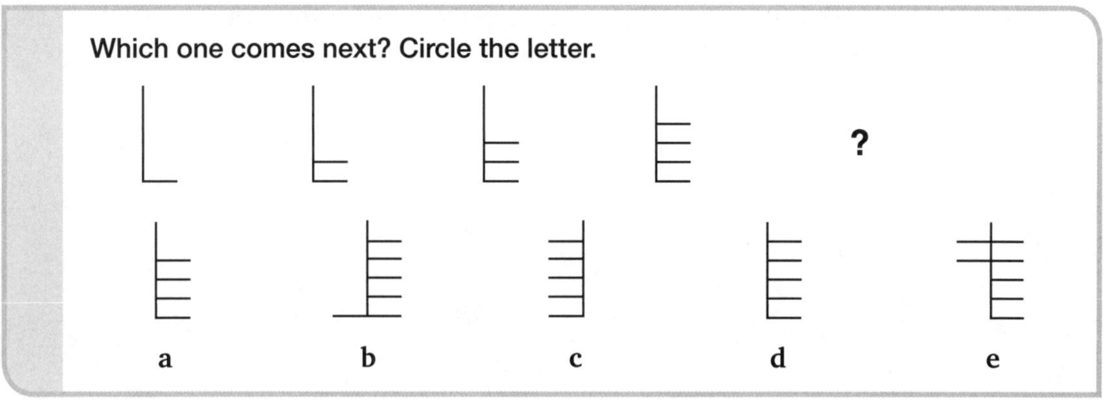

In this sequence it is clear that:

- Each symbol has one vertical line and some horizontal lines.
- The vertical line is the same length in each symbol.
- The horizontal lines are the same length in each symbol.
- All the horizontal lines point to the right.

It seems easy to see then, that the only difference relates to the number of horizontal lines in each step of the sequence.

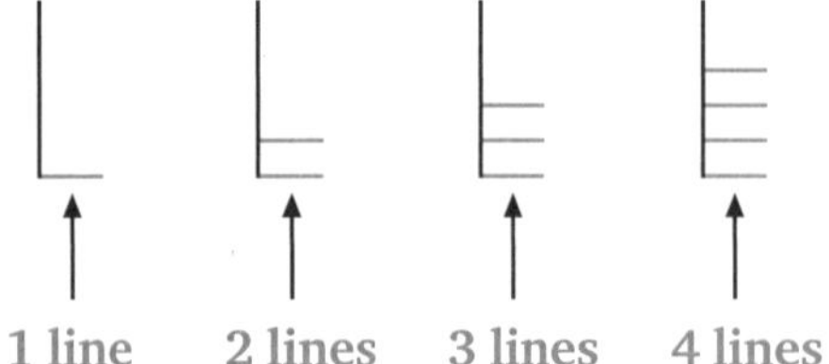

The number of horizontal lines increases by one in each step of the sequence.

Now compare the answer options with this rule and the common features listed above.

Options **b**, **c** and **e** can be eliminated quickly, as they have horizontal lines pointing to the left.

This leaves option **a**: and option **d**:

The last step in the given sequence has four horizontal lines. As the number of lines increases by one each time, the next step must have five lines. Option d is therefore the correct answer.

The next example is based on another element that you may find at the root of many sequence questions. It is often quite easy to see changes to this feature but be careful, it may not be the only rule that applies in a sequence!

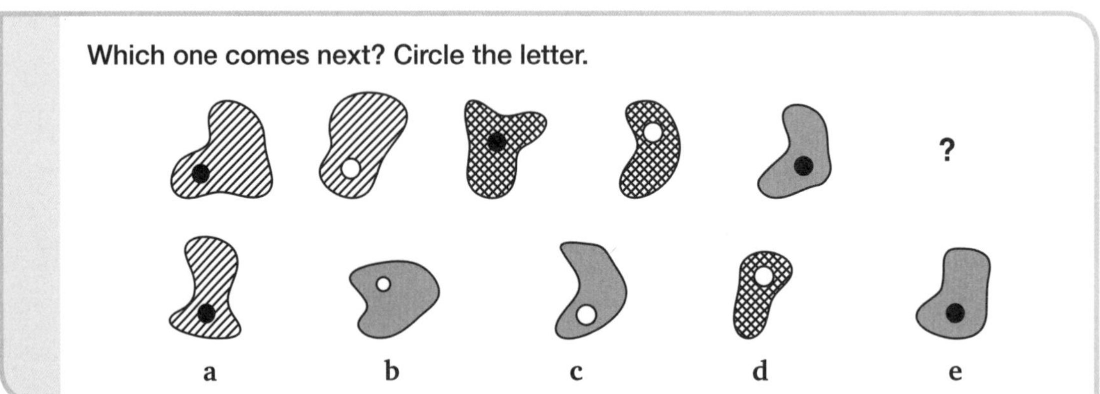

REMEMBER!

With questions that look very simple, it is easy to make a careless mistake. For instance, if you glance at the answer options too quickly in this example, you could choose option c just because it has five horizontal lines, without thinking about direction. Remember that answer options often have very subtle differences, so look very carefully at all elements.

As for the other types of sequence questions, think about what first strikes you about these symbols:

- Each symbol is a different shape and size.
- Each large shape is shaded in some way.
- Each large shape has a circle inside it.
- Each circle is the same size.

Now look at how each step compares with the next:

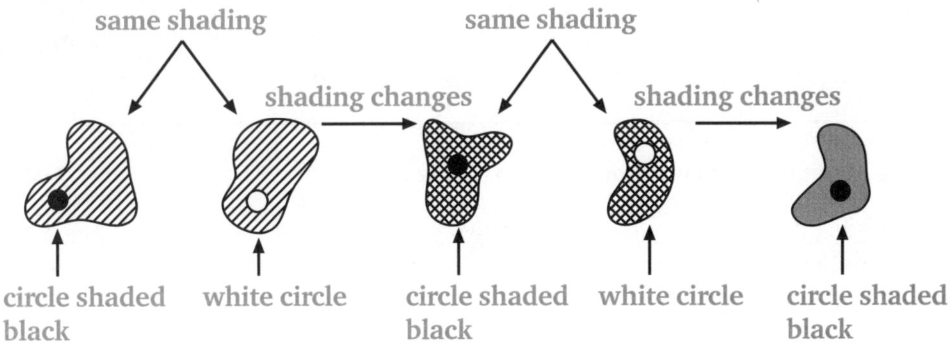

The rule behind this sequence is clearly related to shading and seems to have two aspects:

1 The shading of the large shape is grouped in pairs; the first and second symbols have the same background shading; the third and fourth share the same background shading and so on.
2 The shading of the small inner circle alternates between steps, changing from black to white.

Based on these points, it is possible to conclude that the next symbol in the sequence must:

- have a solid dark grey background – this eliminates options **a** and **d**
- contain a white circle – this eliminates option **e**.

Look carefully at the two remaining options; how do they differ?

REMEMBER!

If you have trouble working out the links in a question, remember to use SPANSS!

The inner circle in option c is the same size as those in the given sequence, so this must be the answer.

Here is the last example of a sequence question. Although a different feature forms the base for this type of sequence, you can use the same strategies and techniques to find the missing step.

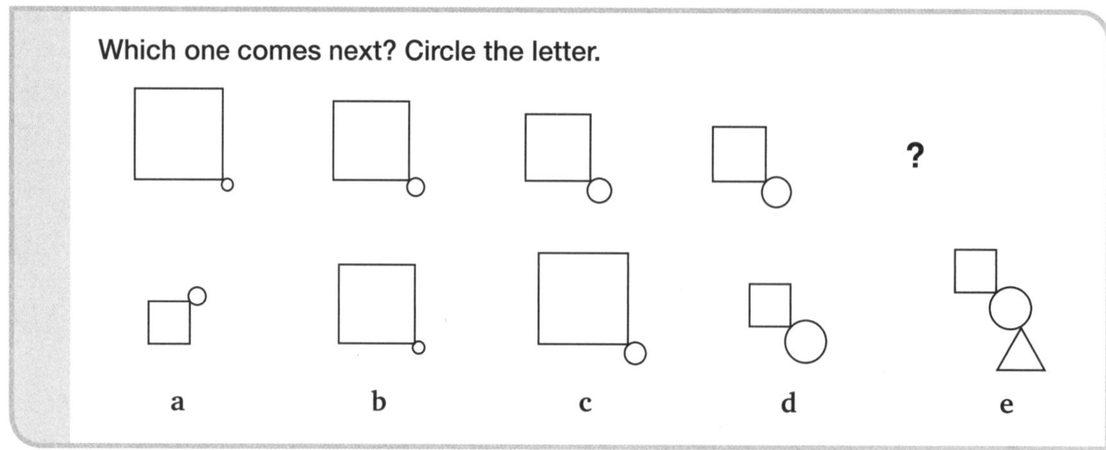

What do you notice about the symbols that make up this sequence?

- Each symbol is made up of a circle and a square only.
- The square gets smaller with each step.
- The circle gets larger with each step.
- The circle is always attached to the square at the bottom right-hand corner.
- There is no shading.

You can now use these observations to make a quick correct option checklist.

The next symbol must have:

- a square smaller than in the fourth step
- a circle larger than in the fourth step
- a circle at the bottom right-hand corner of the square
- no shading
- no other shapes present.

Look at the answer options given. None of them contain any shading, so you can now compare each of the options against the remaining four points on the correct option checklist:

Option	Smaller square?	Larger circle?	Circle at bottom right-hand corner?	No other shapes?
a	✓	✗	—	—
b	✗	—	—	—

Option	Smaller square?	Larger circle?	Circle at bottom right-hand corner?	No other shapes?
c	✗	—	—	—
d	✓	✓	✓	✓
e	✓	✓	✓	✗

From this grid, it is clear that there is only one option that matches all of the elements. Option d must be the next step in the sequence.

> **REMEMBER!**
> As soon as you can eliminate an option, cross it out and move on.

5 *Find a given part within a shape*

The question types in this group are often referred to as **hidden shapes** questions. They test your recognition of shapes or patterns when they are placed within larger symbols. As you do not have to work out a rule or try to find the odd one out in a group of symbols, you may feel this question type is quite straightforward. Some versions of hidden shapes questions can appear easy. However, elements such as shading or a complex shape structure can make this type more difficult to solve. Here we will look at two examples, one straightforward and one that may initially appear more complex.

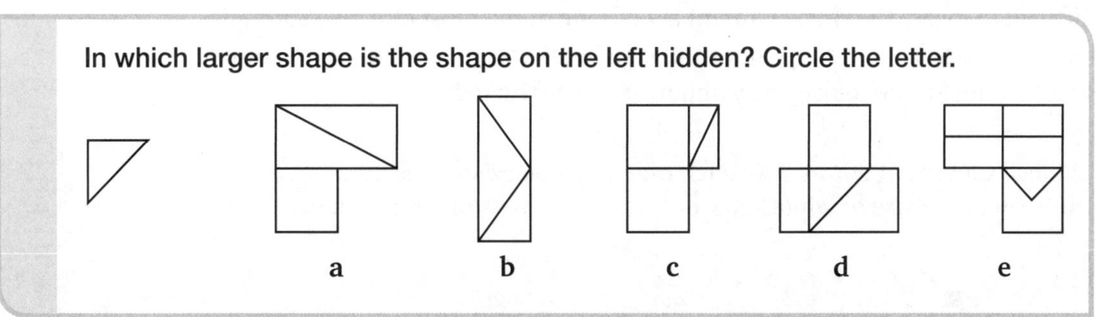

First, make sure you know what you are looking for. In this example, you need to find:

a small right-angled triangle with two sides of equal length.

Now, examine each of the options in turn and highlight any triangles within the symbols.

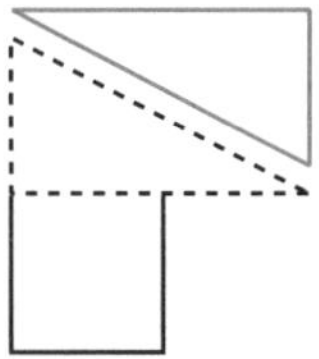  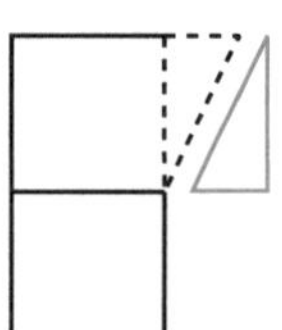 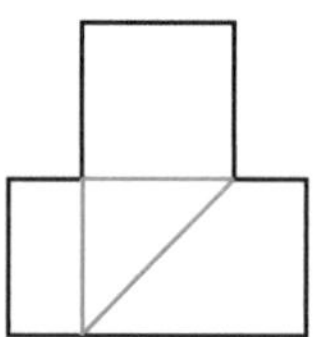 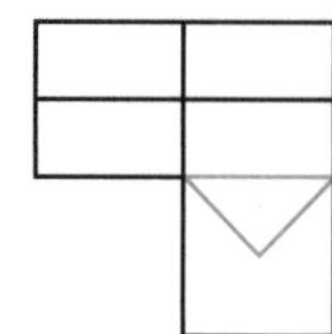

Which options contain a right-angled triangle with two sides of equal length? Options **d** and **e**.

Now compare these two right-angled triangles. Are they the same as the given triangle?

Remember, you must find an exact match in size, shape, shading, angle etc.

Given triangle:

Triangle in option **d**: 

Triangle in option **e**: 

It is now easy to see that option d has the given triangle hidden in its structure.

Now look at an example that may not be so easy to see.

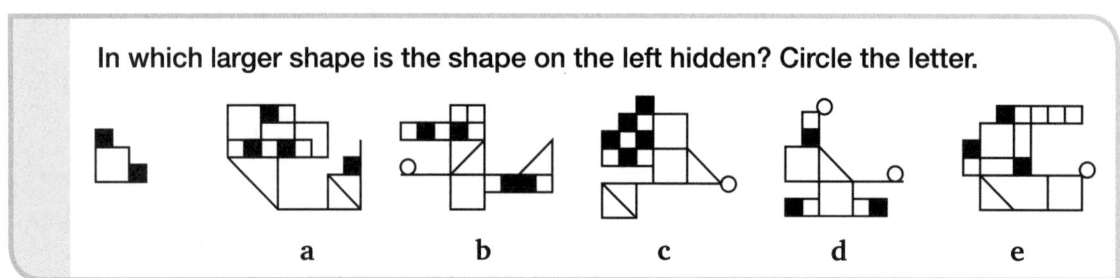

As the given shape and all of the options here have shaded areas, it is more difficult to locate the shape straight away. One of the most effective strategies for this type of hidden shape question is to break the given shape down into smaller chunks and look closely at how it is constructed:

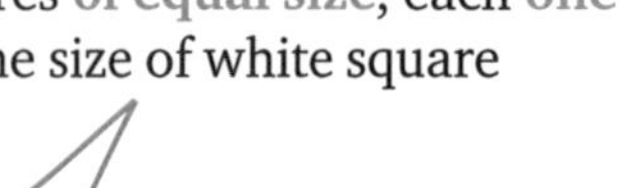

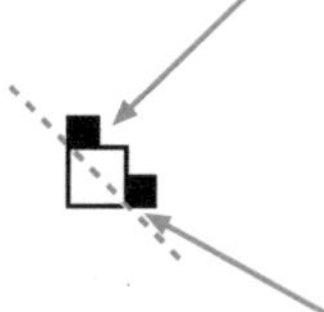

Now follow a methodical approach, looking for these elements in the given options one at a time.

First, look for all of the large white squares in the options.

Then highlight any that have two small black squares attached at corners.

Option **b** contains two large white squares and option **d** has two large white squares but none of these have two black squares attached at corners. These options can therefore be discounted.

This leaves:

Option **a**

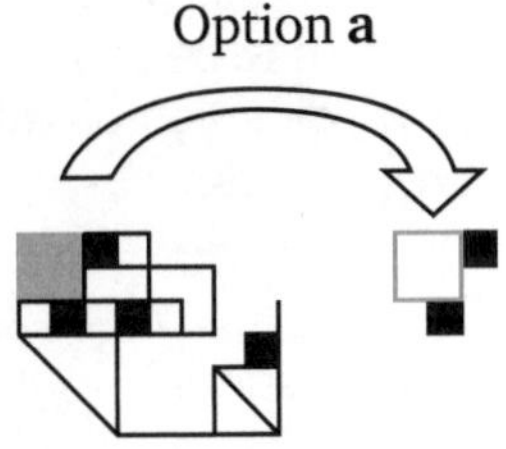

You may be able to see another two large white squares in this pattern but neither of these squares has two black squares attached.

Option **c**

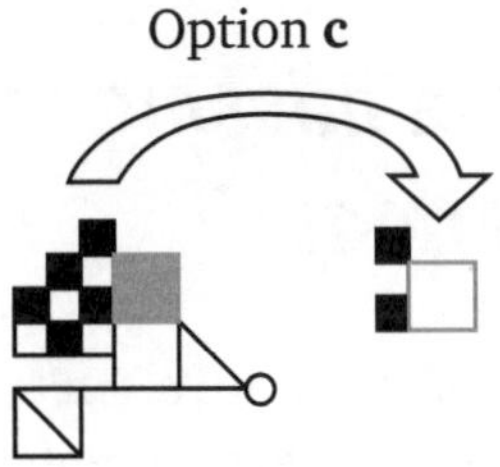

There are two further large white squares here but these do not have two black squares attached at the corners.

Option **e**

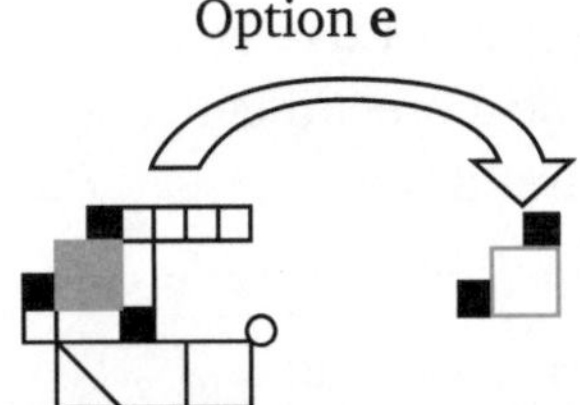

There is one more large square in this pattern but it is not attached to any black squares.

Which of these hidden shapes matches the given shape?

Given shape

Option **a**

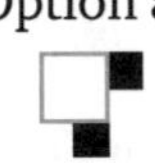

Option **c**

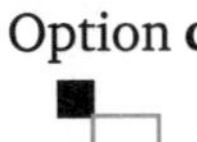

Option **e**

Again, making notes in a grid about the correct option criteria can be useful here.

Criteria	Option a	Option c	Option e
1 large white square	✓	✓	✓
2 black squares of equal size; each one quarter of the size of white square	✓	✓	✓
Black squares on adjacent edges of white square	✓	✗	✓
Black squares attached to diagonally opposite corners of white square	✗	—	✓

From the notes in the grid it seems that option e must be the answer, but it looks different from the given shape. If you are unsure if a symbol is the same, think about what the given shape would look like if it were rotated.

This is how the given shape in the example would look rotated around 360 degrees:

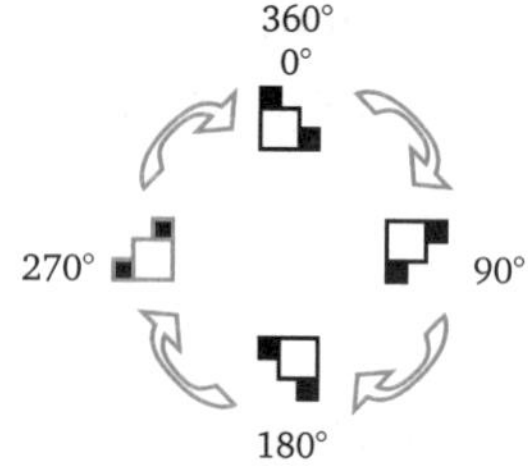

Option e is the same as the given shape, rotated 270 degrees clockwise (or 90 degrees anticlockwise). It is therefore the correct answer.

REMEMBER!

Other shapes may overlap the hidden shape. The given shape may be in a different direction once it's hidden.

6 Find a missing shape from a pattern

These question types are often referred to as matrix (or matrices) questions as the patterns here are presented in the form of a grid. They may seem more complex as, unlike in other non-verbal reasoning questions, the patterns or symbols in matrices are not shown in a straight line.

However, a matrix question is usually based on one or more of the links we have already explored in relation to similarities, analogies and sequences. Some, such as those based on repetition, may be quite straightforward to see, while other patterns, such as those formed by rotation, may be more difficult. If you approach each matrix question in a methodical and careful way, breaking each grid down into smaller chunks, it will be easier to find the rule.

The following examples show four of the most common rules that a matrix question can be based on. As matrix grids can be different sizes, two examples show grids with nine sections and two use grids of four sections. Start by looking at one of the most straightforward versions of matrices.

Which shape or pattern completes the larger square? Circle the letter.

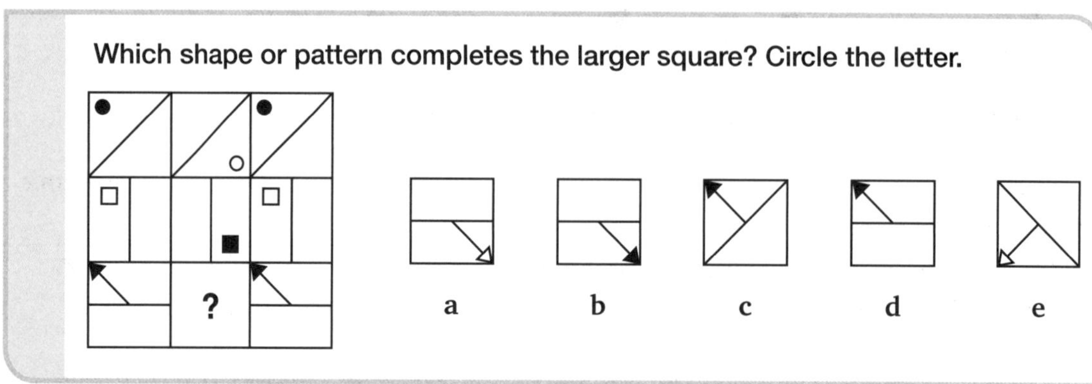

Are there any general things that strike you about the grid?

- The grid has three rows and three columns.
- Each row looks different.
- The first and the third columns look the same.
- There are nine squares.
- Each square contains a line and another symbol.
- Each square is divided in half.

None of these observations will immediately help you to identify the missing square, so now break the grid down into chunks.

Look at the top row. There are four features here.

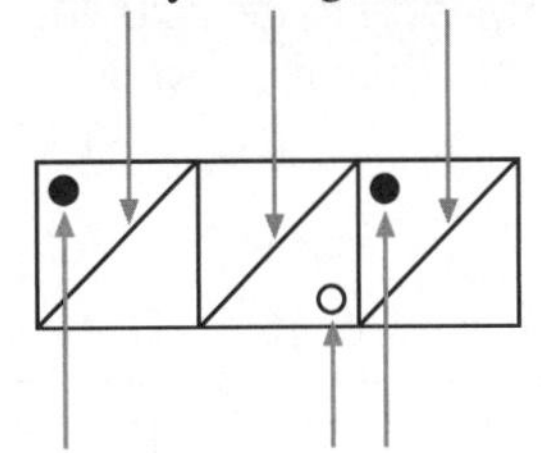

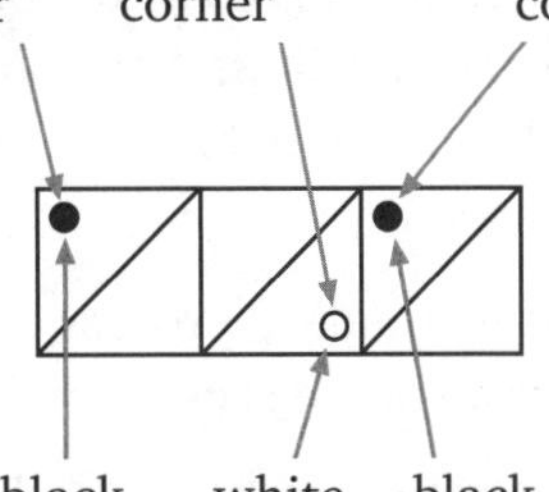

Now look at the given squares in the remaining two rows. Do they have anything in common with the features found in the top row? You may find it helpful to make brief notes in a grid.

	Top row	**Middle row**	**Bottom row**
Each square is divided in half by a:	diagonal line	vertical line	horizontal line
Each square contains:	a small circle	a small square	an arrow
Position of small symbol moves from:	top left – bottom right – top left	top left – bottom right – top left	top left – **?** – top left
Colour of small symbol alternates from:	black – white – black	white – black – white	black – **?** – black

Breaking down the matrix into rows has shown that a **repeating pattern** is forming based on elements of shape, shading and position. We can now use these notes to predict what the missing square in the bottom row will look like.

According to the first two rules indicated above, the missing square must:

- be divided in half by a horizontal line
- contain an arrow.

The third point in the grid shows that the small symbols in the top and middle rows follow the same pattern of movement. The position of the arrow in the two given squares also suggests that the bottom row follows the same alternating pattern. This means that the arrow in the missing square will point to the bottom right corner.

The colour of the small symbols also changes. Looking at the notes in the grid, it is clear that the pattern is alternating from black to white. To complete this pattern, the arrow in the missing square must be white.

REMEMBER!

If you cannot see a pattern in each row, try looking at the features in each column. The rule may apply to the columns rather than the rows.

Now that you have identified the four factors that the missing square must contain, it is easy to look at each of the options and find the correct answer. You can compare the options in a grid if it will help you to focus on the four elements that the answer must have.

Following this methodical process, you should find that option a meets all of the criteria in this example.

To double check that you have chosen the correct option, you could also look at the columns in the grid.

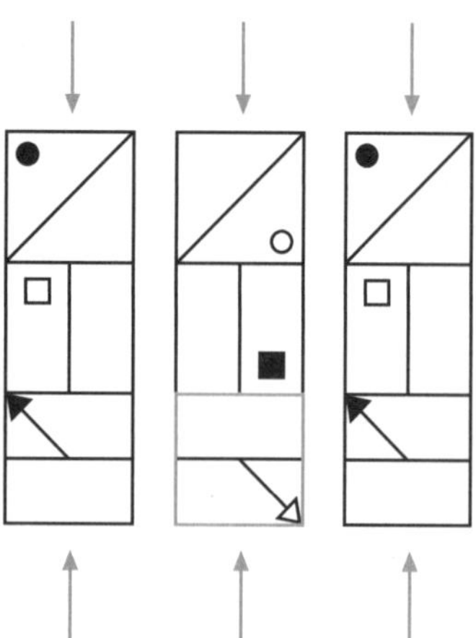

1 Each square is divided in half in a different direction.
2 Each square contains a different symbol.
3 Symbols in the top and bottom squares are the same colour.
4 All symbols are placed in (or point towards) the same corner.

Now look at another example based on a rule that can also be quite easy to spot.

Which shape or pattern completes the larger square? Circle the letter.

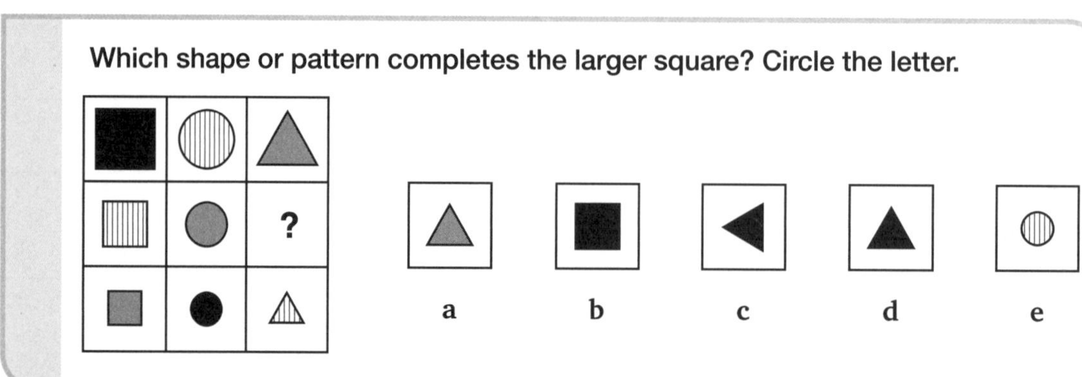

You may be able to see the rule in this type of matrix question straight away, but don't worry if you can't. Follow the same process as before, breaking the matrix down into chunks and looking at it in individual sections.

So for this example, you could first look at each column and describe what you see. Start with the left column:

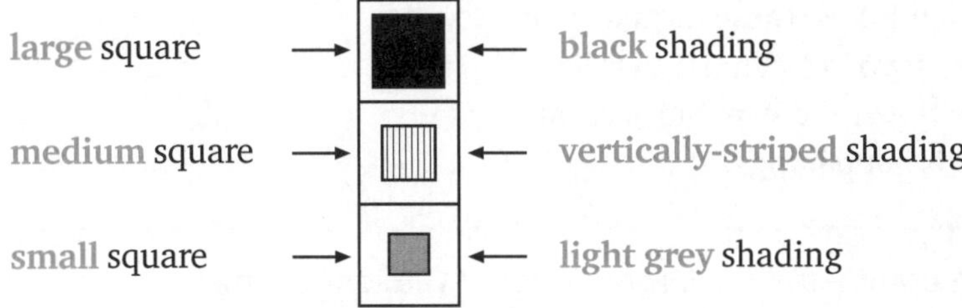

Is a pattern forming? Yes! The first column shows that:

- all boxes show the same symbol
- the symbol decreases in size from the top to the bottom
- each symbol is shaded differently.

Now compare these features with the second column. Does it also follow these rules? Yes, each box shows a circle; the circles decrease in size; each circle is shaded differently.

This confirms that the rule here must be a sequence based on size and shading. It should now be quite straightforward to identify the missing symbol. Remember, making notes in a grid can help you to find the answer quickly.

	Left column	**Middle column**	**Right column**
All boxes shown contain a:	square	circle	triangle
Size of top symbol:	large	large	large
Size of middle symbol:	medium	medium	?
Size of bottom symbol:	small	small	small
Colour of top symbol:	black	vertical stripes	light grey
Colour of middle symbol:	vertical stripes	light grey	?
Colour of bottom symbol:	light grey	black	vertical stripes

From these notes, can you see why the missing square of the matrix will contain a black, medium-sized triangle? Each column has:

- the same shaped symbol in each box – the missing box in the right-hand column must contain a triangle
- a large, medium and small version of the symbol – the right-hand column is missing a medium-sized symbol
- one example of each type of shading – the right-hand column is missing a black symbol.

These criteria mean that options **a**, **b** and **e** can be eliminated.

Both options **c** and **d** show medium-sized black triangles but they look different. Option d must be the answer as it is pointing in the same direction as the other two triangles in the matrix.

> **REMEMBER!**
>
> To check that you have chosen the right option, also look at the pattern in each row.

The next two examples show matrices that are based on more complex rules. Questions that follow these formats may appear more confusing at first but if you remember to follow a methodical approach, breaking the grid down into sections, it will be easier to work out what is happening.

Which shape or pattern completes the larger square? Circle the letter.

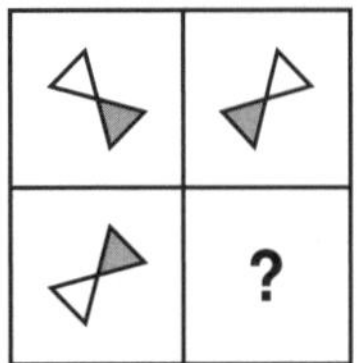

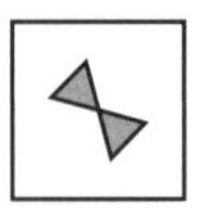

a

b

c

d

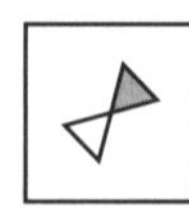

e

It should be clear at a glance that the rule for this matrix is not based on repetition or a sequence. So what is happening here?

The first three notes you might make about this matrix are:

- The grid is divided into quarters.
- Each section of the grid contains the same-shaped symbol.
- The symbol is shaded half grey and half white.

These points will not lead you to the rule, so what else do you notice? Why do none of the three completed sections of the grid look exactly the same? How is the symbol different in each one?

Look at the top half of the grid. In the left section, the white part of the symbol is pointing to the top left-hand corner but in the right section, the white part of the symbol is pointing to the top right-hand corner. Can you think of anything that would cause this change in direction?

Imagine placing a mirror on the dotted line.

What would the mirror image of the symbol look like?

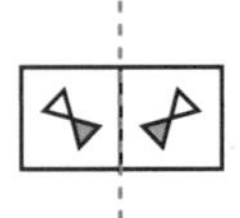

The top right-hand section of the grid is the reflection of the top left-hand section.

Now imagine the mirror runs the full length of the grid.

What would the reflection of the bottom left-hand section look like?

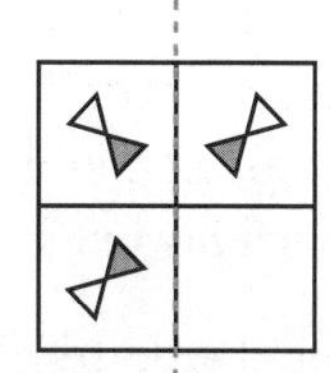

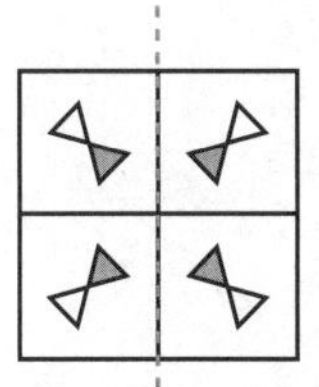

Option d has the symbol in the correct position, so must be the answer.

Only one mirror line has been shown in the explanation of this example but this matrix actually has four lines of symmetry:

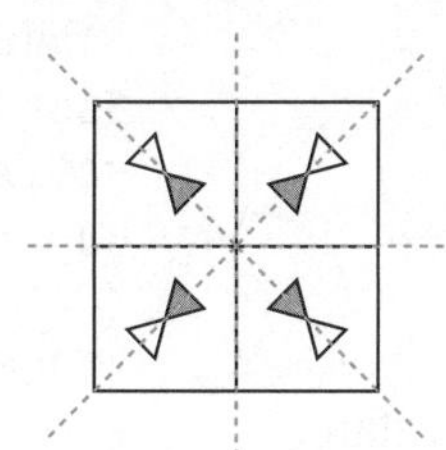

REMEMBER!

If you cannot see a reflection on the first mirror line you try, check all other possible directions.

Any of these lines of symmetry may be applied to reflection matrices. In the case of this example, a mirror placed on any of these lines would give you the same grid design, but this will not always be true.

This next example is based on a rule that can be difficult to see at first. Or you may understand what is happening, but find it hard to visualise the answer. This is because it relies on spatial awareness.

Which shape or pattern completes the larger square? Circle the letter.

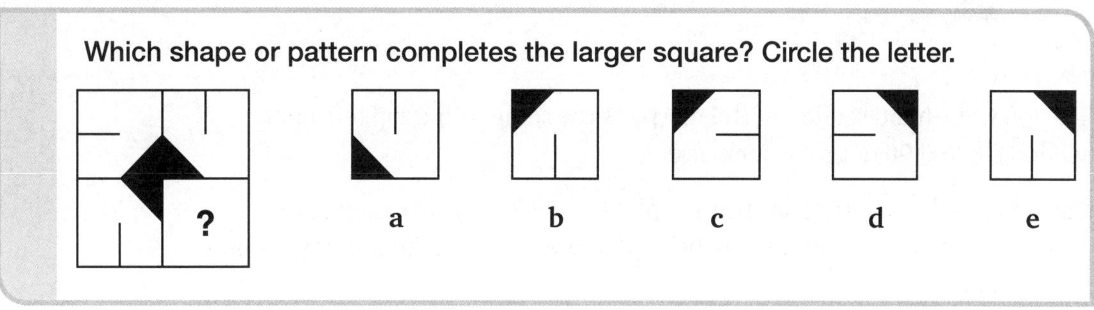

Your first thought could be that this is a reflection question, but a quick assessment to check mirror lines will discount this.

So, first, describe what you can see:

- The grid is divided into quarters.
- Each section contains a short line.
- Each section contains a small, black, right-angled triangle.
- The black triangles appear to form three sides of a square.

As before, break the matrix down into four parts and look at how pairs of sections relate to each other.

Look at the two left-hand sections of the matrix. In the bottom left-hand section the short line is at the bottom of the box and is in a vertical position. In the top left-hand section, the short line is on the left-hand side of the box and is in a horizontal position. What could cause the line to change direction?

Imagine the bottom left-hand section is turned 90 degrees clockwise. What would it look like?

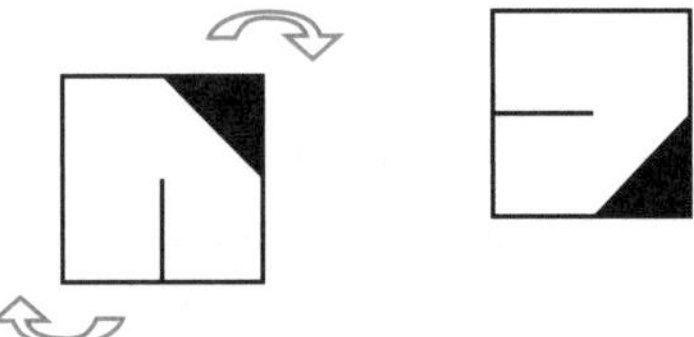

REMEMBER!

If you have difficulty visualising what a shape or symbol will look like when it is rotated clockwise or anticlockwise, try turning the paper round in that direction.

The top left-hand section of the matrix is the same as the bottom left-hand section rotated 90 degrees clockwise.

Now look at the top right-hand section. How does this relate to the top left-hand section of the grid?

What would the top left-hand section look like if it was also rotated 90 degrees clockwise?

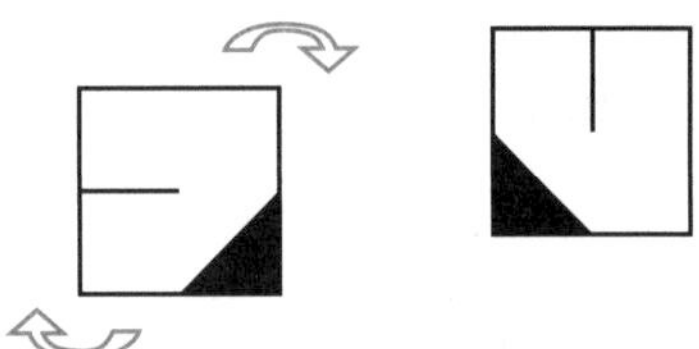

The top right-hand section of the matrix is the same as the top left-hand section rotated 90 degrees clockwise.

Can you see the rule that has been applied here? This is an example of a **rotation** matrix. You should now be able to predict what the missing section will look like.

Think about what the top right-hand section would look like rotated 90 degrees clockwise.

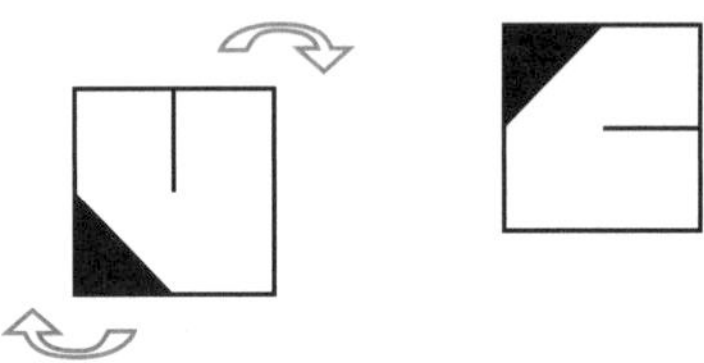

Option **c** is the only possible answer.

Rotating shapes

We have already seen how reflection and rotation can form the basis of a range of non-verbal reasoning question types. This group is based fully around these elements, testing your:

- understanding of symmetry
- knowledge of 3D shapes
- spatial awareness.

The approach to the questions in this group is slightly different, as you do not need to work out the link between a set of symbols. You will already know from reading the question instructions what rule has been applied to the given shape and the answer options.

There are two main sets of rotating shapes questions:

- Recognise mirror images
- Link nets to cubes

Exam tips

To help you identify the answer quickly in an exam, try sketching your predicted reflection. Remember that the reflected image will be the same distance from the mirror line as the original shape, just in the opposite direction. When it comes to linking cubes and nets, remember that opposite faces will never be adjacent on the net – quickly checking this before anything else will allow you to reject some options immediately.

We'll start by looking at mirror images.

7 *Recognise mirror images*

This set of questions is often referred to as **reflected shapes**. This type tests your understanding of symmetry and to work out these questions you have to visualise shapes in a new plane. The actual size or number of parts of the given symbol will not change but elements of the mirror image could appear in a different direction or angle and may have changes to shading.

Reflected shapes questions can appear quite straightforward, as you do not have to work out a common link between a set of symbols, imagine a rotated form, or locate a particular section hidden within another symbol. However, subtle differences in the structure or shading of some answer options can catch you out. It is easy to make a careless mistake with this type of question, so you need to apply expert observation skills.

You may be able to see the mirror image of a reflected shape straight away but don't worry if you can't. If you remember some key points and follow a logical thought process, you will be able to identify the answer. Look at the following two examples of typical mirror image questions, as well as a range of strategies for practising this question type.

Which shape on the right is the reflection of the shape given on the left? Circle the letter.

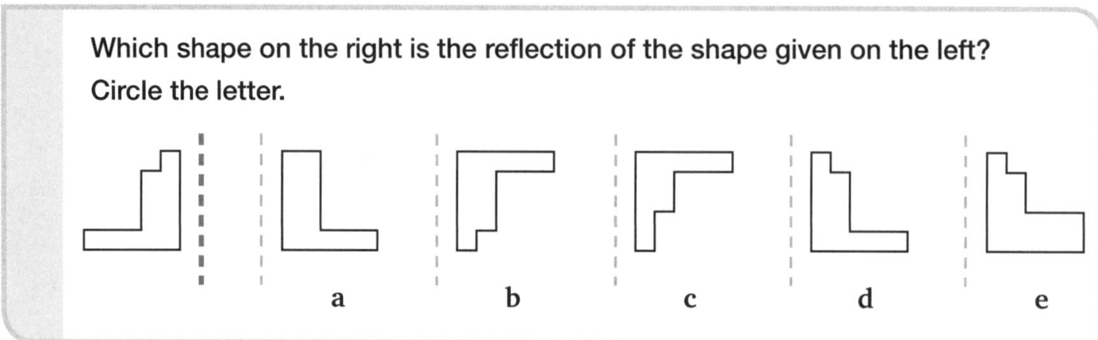

As shown in this example, most reflection questions will place the given shape on one side of a dotted line. This dotted line represents the line of reflection or line of symmetry.

Before you can find the reflection, you must first familiarise yourself with the given symbol.

How would you describe its basic shape?
Does it have any noticeable features?
How many corners or curves does it have?
Does it have any shaded areas?

You might think that the image in this example reminds you of a set of steps as it has some parts 'cut out' on the left-hand side. You might also notice that it has eight corners and no shading.

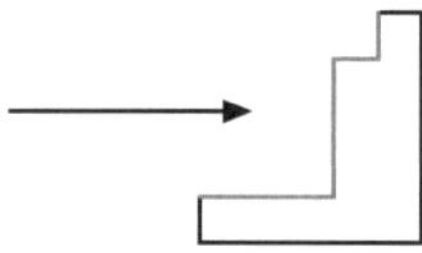

Next, break the shape down into sections and try to imagine a mirror along the line of symmetry. What would the reflection of each part look like?

Here are some of the elements you could consider for any given symbol:

What part of the symbol is closest to or furthest away from the mirror?
Would the horizontal lines change position or direction?
Would the vertical lines change position or direction?
Would the diagonal lines change position or direction?
What would happen to the curved sections?
How might the direction of any other features (such as arrowheads) change?
Is there any shading that would look different?

REMEMBER!

Thinking about these types of questions may help you eliminate options straight away.

So for this example you might note that:

The small 'step' is at the top of the shape.

This edge is closest to the mirror.

This edge is furthest from the mirror.

The long 'step' is at the bottom of the shape.

REMEMBER!

Once you are familiar with the given shape, you may find it helpful to quickly sketch what you think the reflection will look like before you look at the options.

Keeping these points in mind, as well as your initial thoughts about the shape, it should now be much easier to compare it with the options to find the right reflection. Make brief notes in a grid if it helps.

	Option a	Option b	Option c	Option d	Option e
Looks like steps?	✗	✓	✓	✓	✓
Small step at the top?	—	✗	✗	✓	✓
Long step at the bottom?	—	—	—	✓	✓

Options **a**, **b** and **c** can be eliminated at this point as they do not meet the criteria.

This leaves options **d** and **e**. Compare these two images with the given shape. Which is the mirror image?

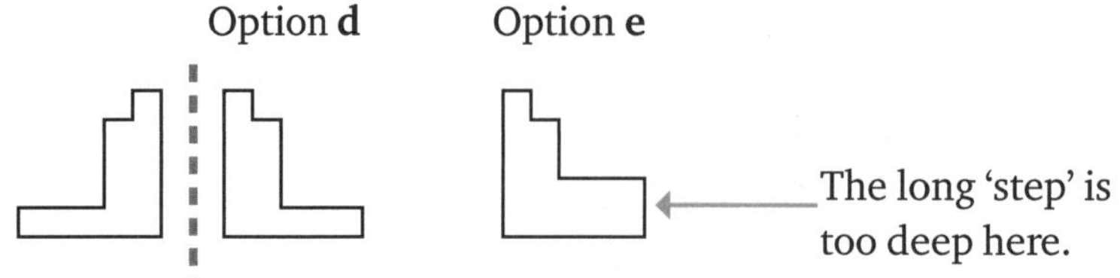

Following this methodical thought process, it is clear that the answer to this example is option d.

REMEMBER!

If you have difficulty imagining a mirror on the line of reflection, try thinking of the given shape as a pattern that has been drawn in ink. If you folded the piece of paper along the dotted line and over the shape, what image would be transferred onto the other side of the paper?

This line drawing was an example of a simple mirror image question. Now look at another example that may appear more complicated but which can be solved by following the same logical, step-by-step technique.

Which shape on the right is the reflection of the shape given on the left? Circle the letter.

a b c d e

When symbols are made up of several components it is easy to get confused or to overlook a feature when trying to compare the given shape with the possible reflections. Don't panic! Just break the symbol down into manageable chunks and look at these in turn.

What initial observations can you make about this shape?

The central section of the shape looks like it forms three parts of a cross.

The small black square is furthest away from the line of reflection at the top of the shape.

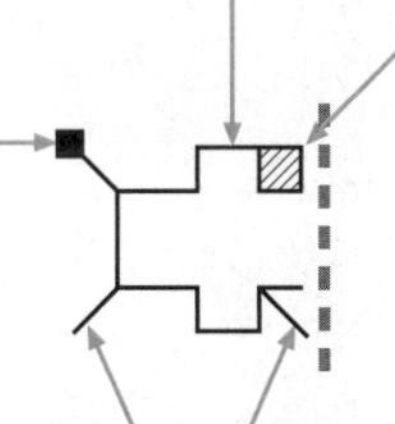

The diagonally-striped square is closest to the line of reflection at the top of the shape.

The two short diagonal lines at the bottom of the shape point in opposite directions.

REMEMBER!

When looking at the specific features of the given shape, think about their positions in relation to the mirror line. Their reflections will be the same distance from the mirror, just in the opposite direction.

With these elements in mind, look at each of the options quickly. Can any of them be immediately discounted? Yes, option **e** – here the small black square is next to the mirror line.

Now look at the remaining four options more closely and compare them with your notes about the given shape.

Central section looks like three parts of a cross	✓	✓	✓	✓
Diagonally-striped square next to mirror line	✓	✗	✓	✓
Two short diagonal lines at bottom, pointing in opposite directions	✓	—	✓	✓

The reflection is either option **a**, **c** or **d**.

This is where your attention to detail is very important. You now need to look very closely and compare every aspect of each pattern to work out how they differ.

Option a

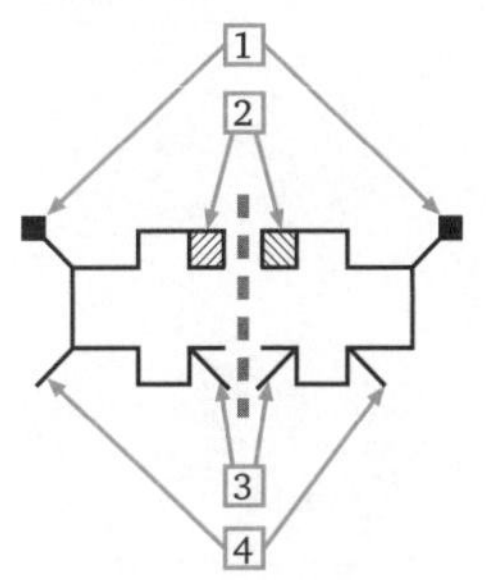

1 Small black square in correct position. ✓

2 Striped shading in correct direction. ✓

3 Short diagonal line in correct position and direction. ✓

4 Second diagonal line in correct position. ✗

Option **a** cannot be the answer.

Option c

1 Small black square in correct position. ✓

2 Striped shading in correct direction. ✓

3 Short diagonal line in correct position and direction. ✓

4 Second diagonal line in correct position and direction. ✓

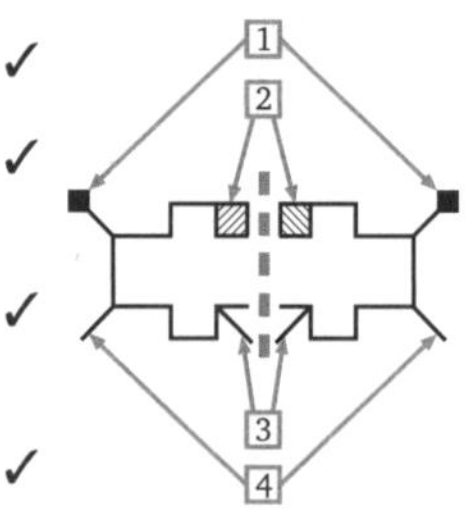

Option **c** appears to have all of the elements in the correct positions but check option **d** quickly just to be sure!

Option d

1 Small black square in correct position. ✓

2 Striped shading in correct direction. ✗

There is no need to continue the comparison as the diagonally-striped shading has not been reflected. Option **d** cannot be the answer.

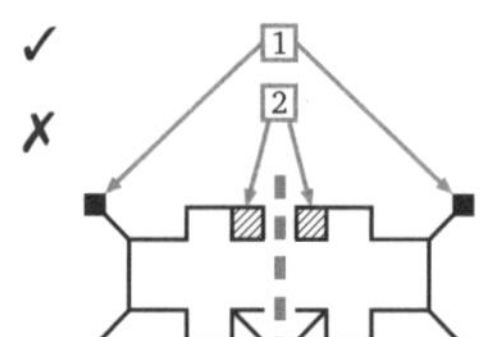

This confirms that option **c** shows the reflection of this complex shape.

> REMEMBER!
>
> If you want to see what happens to different types of shapes when they are reflected, draw a range of shapes and place a mirror next to them. Or draw over the shapes with tracing paper and, without rotating it, flip the tracing paper over horizontally and see what happens to each shape. The more familiar you are with how shapes do or don't change when reflected, the easier these questions will become.

> REMEMBER!
>
> A mirror line might not always be to the right of the given shape. It may be on the left or above or below the original symbol, so pay close attention to the direction in which the shape is being reflected. Wherever the mirror line is, you can still use the techniques shown here to find the reflection.

8 *Link nets to cubes*

The questions in this group are called **nets** and they test your spatial awareness. Many people struggle with this type of question as you have to think in three-dimensional terms. You need to be able to relate a two-dimensional outline, or net, to a three-dimensional shape and this can be hard to visualise.

There are 11 different ways that a cube can be cut to make a net. However, it is unlikely that you will need to be familiar with all of these versions for non-verbal reasoning as these questions often only involve three styles of net: the vertical cross, the horizontal cross and the T-shape.

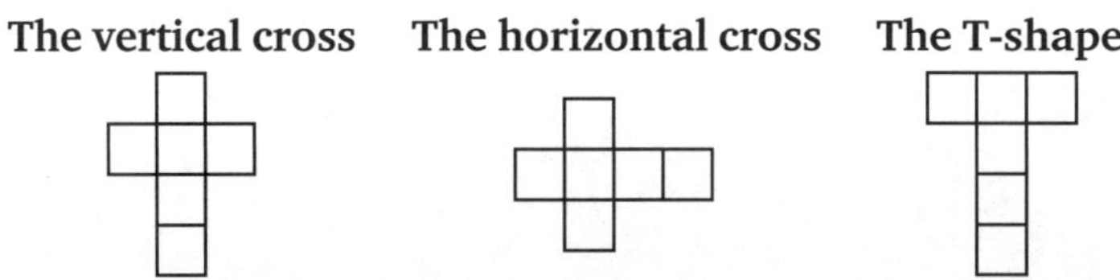

Whatever style of net a question is based on, there are some basic rules that can help you visualise any net as a solid cube. First, we'll explore these rules in relation to the vertical cross.

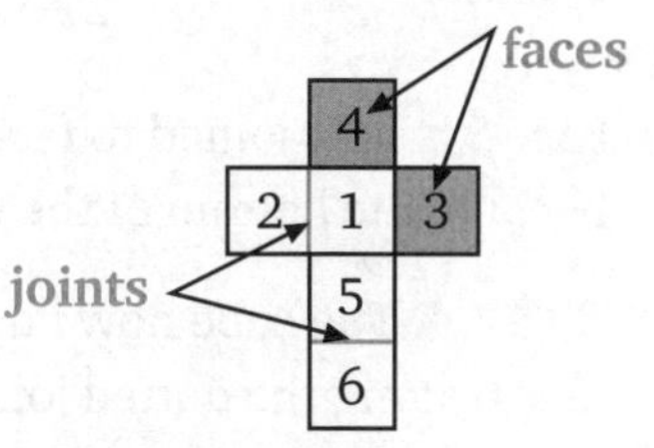

a Try to think of a cube as having four sides, a top and a bottom. Each of these is represented by one of the six **faces** that form the net. These faces are connected by five **joints**. When the net is folded, these joints will become five out of the 12 **edges** of the cube.

This leaves seven edges, which are created as the cube is formed. These edges are made by folding the net along the joints and joining the faces together. You can think of it as drawing two pieces of material together and sewing a **seam**.

Some of these seams are easier to visualise than others, so we'll start with the more straightforward ones!

REMEMBER!

Depending on how you fold a net, any face can be viewed as the top, side or bottom of the cube.

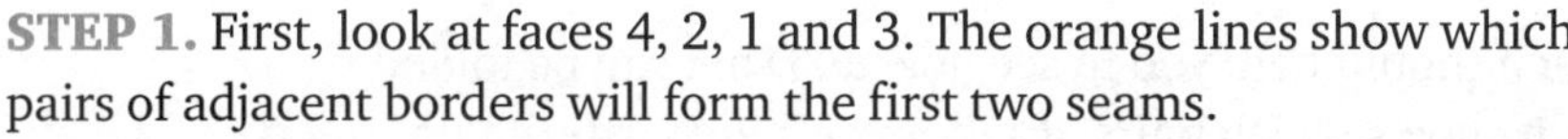

STEP 1. First, look at faces 4, 2, 1 and 3. The orange lines show which pairs of adjacent borders will form the first two seams.

Imagine folding face 4 along the dotted joint to make this face the top of the cube.

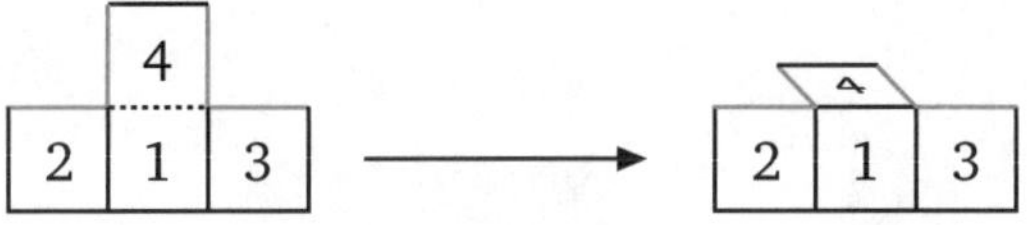

STEP 2. Now imagine folding faces 2 and 3 along the dotted joints. Face 4 is now joined together with faces 2 and 3, forming two seams or edges of the cube. Faces 1, 2 and 3 have become three sides of the cube.

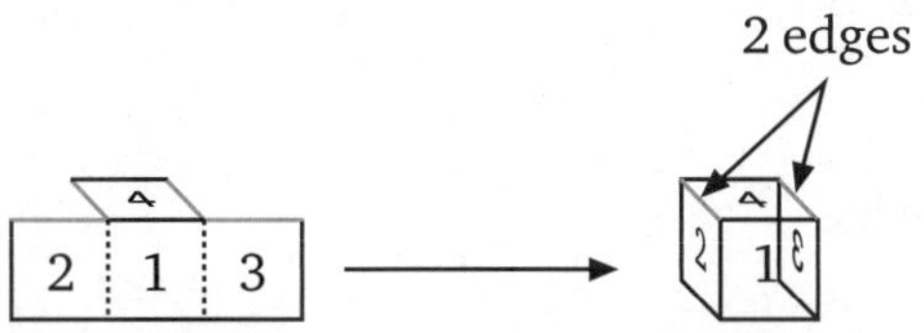

STEP 3. This leaves faces 5 and 6. First, think about folding face 5 along the dotted joint, so it sits underneath the shape. Again, the orange lines show which adjacent borders will meet up.

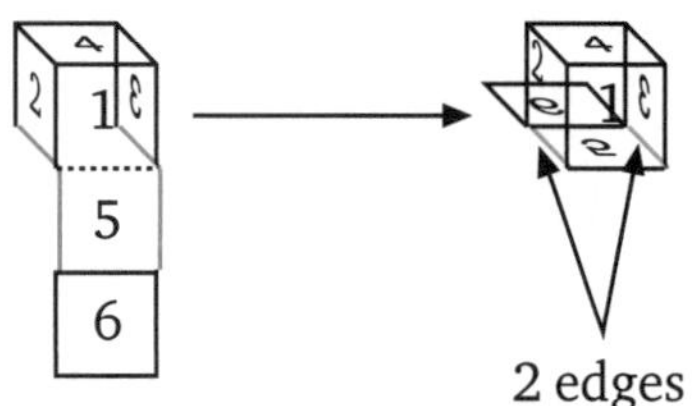

Face 5 is now joined to faces 2 and 3, forming two more edges, and it has become the bottom of the cube.

STEP 4. The cube now has a top, a bottom and three sides. Imagine folding face 6 along the dotted joint so that the three pairs of opposite orange borders meet.

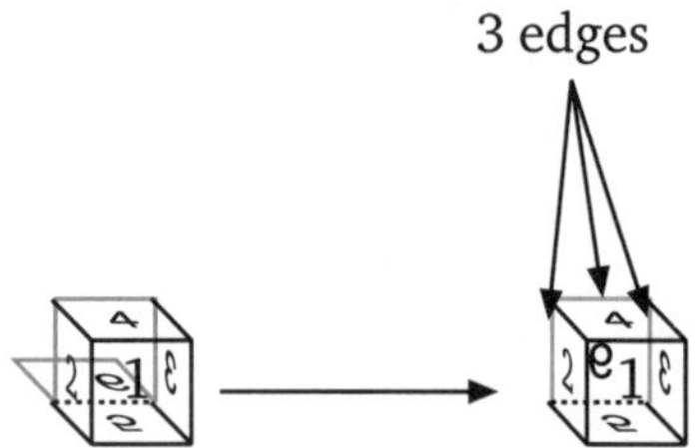

Face 6 is now joined with face 4 and has formed the last three edges of the cube. The net has now become a cube.

This stepped approach should help you to see how a 2D net can be folded to create a 3D cube. It shows which pairs of **adjacent face borders join together** to make the missing seven edges of the cube.

b Now look at the next rule that can help you to visualise how a net can become a 3D shape.

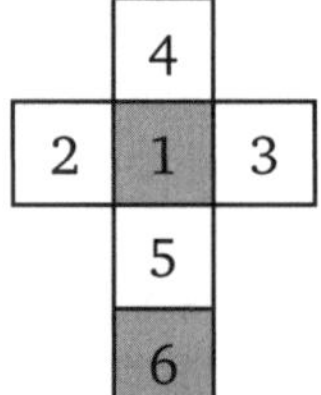

REMEMBER!

Faces that are connected by joints in a net will always be next to each other in a cube.

Two faces in each of these nets have been shaded.

What do you notice about the positions of these pairs of faces in the cubes?

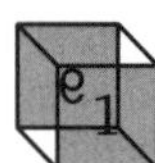

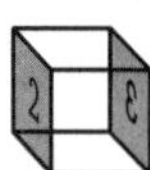

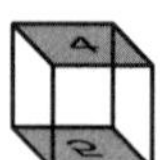

Alternate faces in a net end up opposite each other when folded into a cube so, using the numbering system shown for the vertical cross:

- Face 1 will always be opposite face 6.
- Face 2 will always be opposite face 3.
- Face 4 will always be opposite face 5.

c There is one more rule you need to think about when solving net questions and it can be the trickiest to visualise as it involves your understanding of rotation.

When imagining how a net will fold up to make a cube, you need to think about whether the direction or orientation of any symbols will change as each face is folded along the joints.

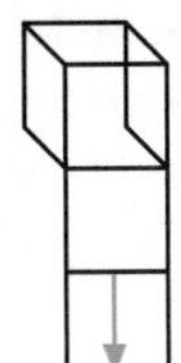

To help, put a symbol onto the net, starting with face 6. Here is the net again at Step 3 in **a** above.

What do you think will happen to the arrow as face 6 is folded to form the back of the cube? Look at Steps 3 and 4 again. What do you notice?

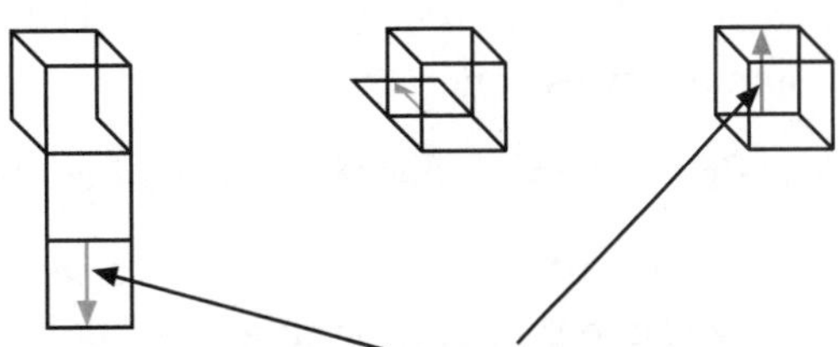

As face 6 has been folded to meet face 4, the direction of the arrow has changed. In the completed cube the arrow appears to be reversed, now pointing up instead of down.

For the next example it is helpful to compare a section of the vertical cross with a section of the T-shaped net.

Here are faces 4, 2 and 1 of the vertical cross as seen at Step 2 in **a** above.

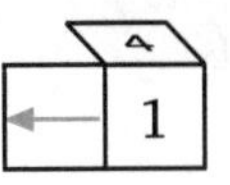

Do you think the orientation of the arrow will change as face 2 is folded to meet face 4?

No, the direction of the horizontal arrow has not changed as face 2 has been folded.

Now look at what happens when face 2 is folded in the T-shape.

2	4	3
	1	
	5	
	6	

As in the vertical cross, faces 2, 4 and 1 are connected, but here it is the adjacent borders of face 2 and face 1 that meet.

Now imagine that face 4 is folded along the dotted joint, forming the top of the cube.

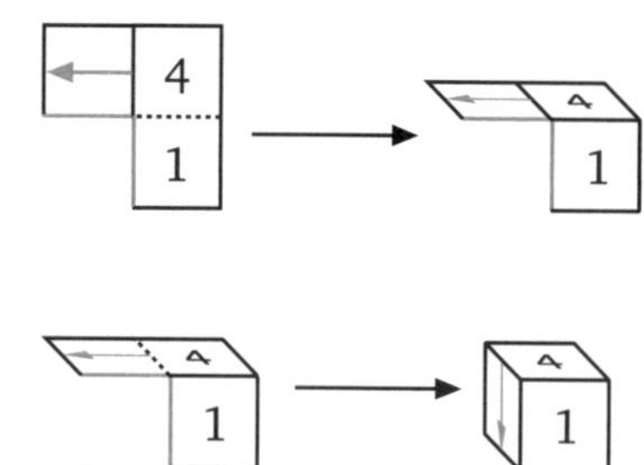

You can also place a horizontal arrow on face 2 as before.

After this move the arrow is still in a horizontal position.

Now visualise folding face 2 along the dotted joint, so that it meets face 1 and forms a seam, or an edge of the cube.

What has happened to the orientation of the arrow?

With the second fold, the direction of the arrow appears to have changed. The horizontal arrow has become vertical.

These two stepped examples show that:

- **a symbol on the net face that forms the back of the cube when folded may become reversed**
- **a symbol on a face that is folded more than once may change its orientation.**

Now that we have looked at the rules that can help solve net questions, look at three worked examples using each of the common styles of net.

The first example is based on the vertical cross.

This version of a net question shows a vertical cross and is asking you to find the one cube that cannot be made from this net.

REMEMBER!

One of the best ways to visualise how cubes are made from nets is to actually draw and cut out some nets yourself. Then, number the faces and see what happens as you fold them together along the joints to create the cube. To help you get started, you can find a range of nets for cubes on our website. Just follow the Free Resources link.

Which cube cannot be made from the given net? Circle the letter.

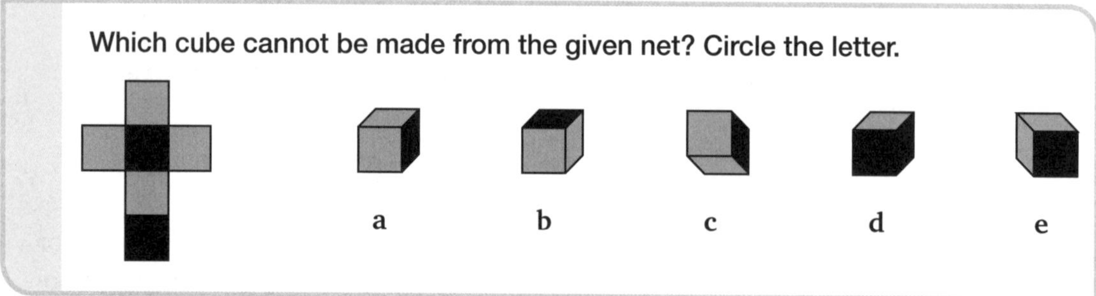

You may be able to see the answer straight away, but if not, work through the three rules and think about the answer options at each stage:

1 **Work out which adjacent borders will meet to form the seams, or edges, of the 3D cube.**

This may not help you to eliminate any options for this example as there are so many faces that have light-grey shading.

REMEMBER!

These three versions of net questions use very similar wording, so read the instructions carefully to make sure you know what you are being asked to do.

2 Identify which faces will be opposite each other when the cube is formed.

When comparing the pairs of opposites with the options, it should be clear that option **d** may be the answer as this shows two adjacent black faces.

Faces 1 and 6 are the only black faces in the net and these would be opposite, not next to each other, when the cube was formed.

3 Look out for any symbols that could be rotated as the faces are folded.

There are no symbols in this net and no shading that could rotate, so this rule does not apply to this example.

Option **d** must therefore be the answer – it cannot be made from the given net as the faces are not shown in the correct positions.

This next example uses the horizontal cross.

Which cube can be made from the given net? Circle the letter.

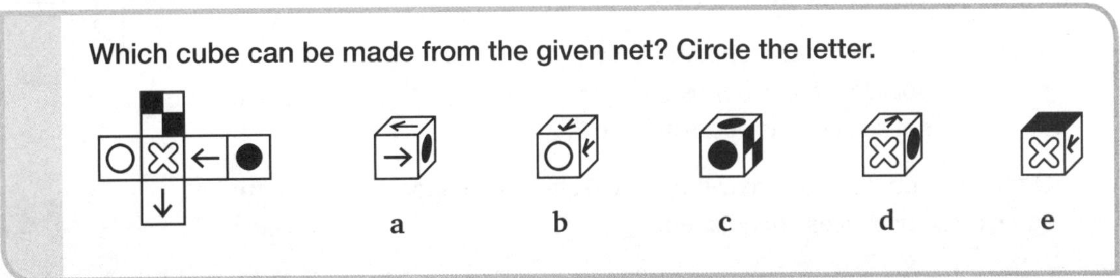

First, make sure you understand what the question is asking. Here you need to find one cube that **can be made** from the net.

Net questions may seem more confusing when they involve symbols. However, there is a quick trick you can try to eliminate some options before you think about the three rules.

Scan each answer option, comparing the symbols or shading that the cubes contain with those in the net. If any cubes have a type of symbol or shading not present in the net, you know that these options cannot be made and can therefore be eliminated.

A quick look at the answer options and the net in this example should show you that options **c** and **e** can be eliminated immediately:

- Option **c** shows two black circles; the net only has one black circle.
- Option **e** shows a top face shaded black; the net does not have a black face.

This leaves options **a**, **b** and **d**, which you can now think about in relation to the three rules.

1 **Work out which adjacent opposite borders will meet to form the seams, or edges, of the 3D cube.**

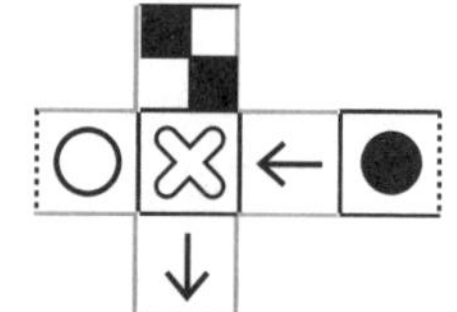

Option **a** could be the answer as the black circle is connected by a joint to the horizontal arrow and it would be joined to the vertical arrow when the adjacent borders met.

Option **b** could be the answer as the white circle would be joined with the vertical arrow when their adjacent borders met.

Option **d** cannot be the answer. The black circle would not be joined to the cross so this can be eliminated.

2 **Identify which faces will be opposite each other when the cube is formed.**

	3		
4	1	5	6
	2		

Option **a** could be the answer as:

- you cannot see what is opposite face 6
- you cannot see what is opposite face 5
- you cannot see what is opposite face 2.

Option **b** cannot be the answer as face 4 should be opposite face 5. In the cube, these two faces are adjacent.

Option **a** seems to be the only possible answer, but double-check this against rule three to be sure.

3 **Look out for any symbols that could be rotated as the faces are folded.**

What would happen to the orientation of the arrows when faces 2, 5 and 6 were folded?

Imagine folding the cube around face 5, making this the top of the cube.

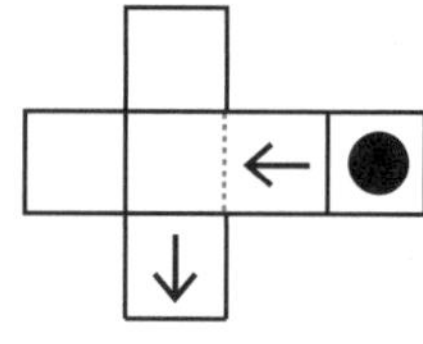

Start by folding the dotted joint between face 1 and face 5.

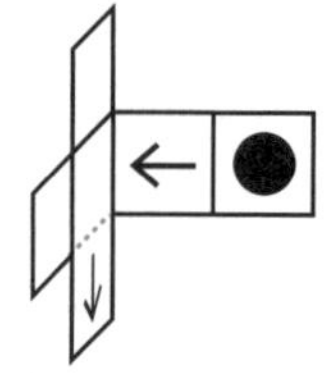

Next, fold face 2 along the dotted joint so it forms a seam with face 5. Notice the change in orientation of the arrow.

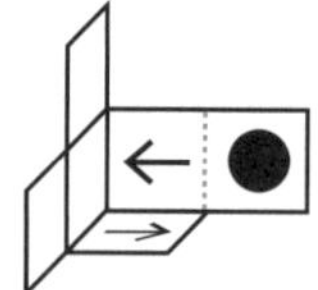

Now fold face 6 so it forms a seam with face 2.

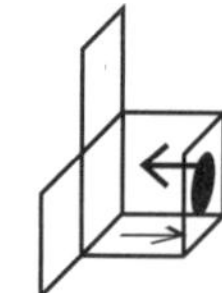

Does this look like option **a**?

Yes.

- The arrow on face 5 is still facing away from the circle on face 6.
- The arrow on face 2 is now horizontal and pointing towards face 6.

Option **a** is the correct answer.

> **REMEMBER!**
> Turning the paper round can often help you imagine what would happen to a face if it were folded along a joint.

The final example is based on the T-shape net and it follows a different format to the other two versions. In this style of net question, you are given a cube and you have to work out which net has been used to create it. You may find this format confusing at first but you can still apply the same rules and step-by-step techniques to work out the answer.

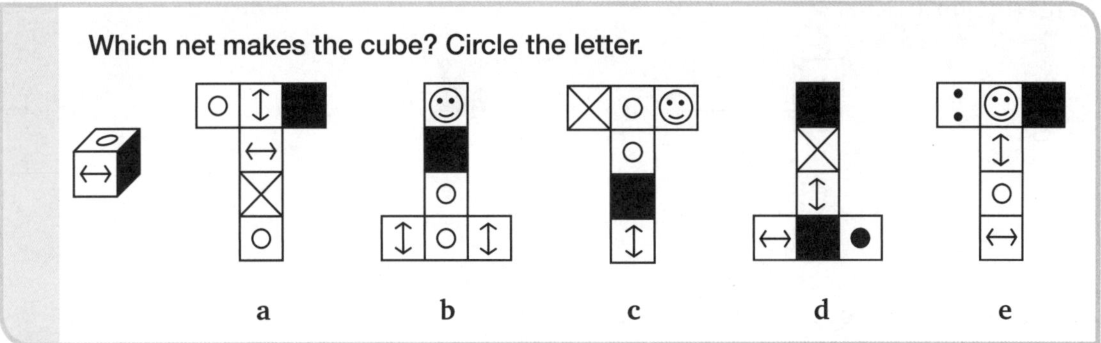

First, scan the nets and check whether any of the options can be eliminated straight away. As you can only see the top and two sides of the cube you do not know what symbols or shading will be on the rest of the faces. You can therefore only eliminate a net at this stage if it does not contain all three of the given cube faces.

Can any nets be eliminated? Yes, option **d**. It does not have a white circle, so it cannot be the answer.

This leaves options **a**, **b**, **c** and **e** to consider in relation to the three rules.

It might be easier to look at option **c** first as this only contains one double-ended arrow, whereas the other three options have two double-ended arrows.

Concentrate on the faces that have the same symbols as shown in the cube. So for option **c** these are faces 4, 1, 5 and 6.

Faces 4 and 1 both show a circle. Think about which one of these could be showing on the top of the cube.

You know that face 1 and face 6 will be opposite each other when the cube is folded. The cube shows the circle and the double-ended arrow on adjacent faces, so face 1 cannot be the top of the cube.

Now look at the second circle. You know that face 4 and face 5 will be opposite each other when the cube is folded. The cube shows the circle and the black shaded side on adjacent faces, so face 4 cannot be the top of the cube.

Option **c** can be discounted. Work through the remaining options from left to right to make sure you look at each one in the same way.

Here is option **a**.

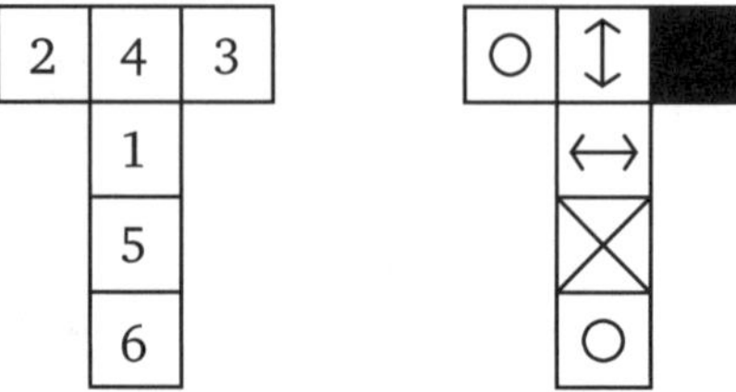

Faces 2 and 3 will be opposite when the net is folded but the cube shows the circle and black shaded side on adjacent faces. The circle on face 2 therefore cannot be on the top of the cube.

Now look at face 6. Faces 1 and 6 will also be opposite when the cube is formed. The double-ended arrow is shown on an adjacent face to the circle in the cube, so the arrow on face 1 cannot be the one shown.

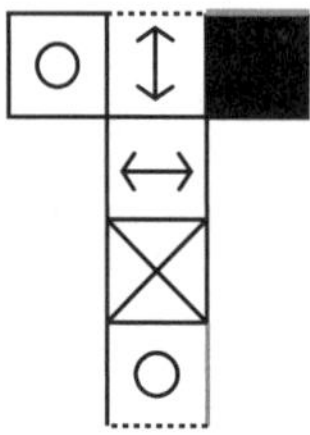

This leaves faces 4, 3 and 6.

Which face borders will face 6 meet when the net is folded? The borders of faces 4, 3 and 6 will meet to create two edges of the cube.

Option **a** could still be the answer. You will need to visualise these faces joining together to be sure.

Imagine folding the cube around face 1, making this the front of the cube.

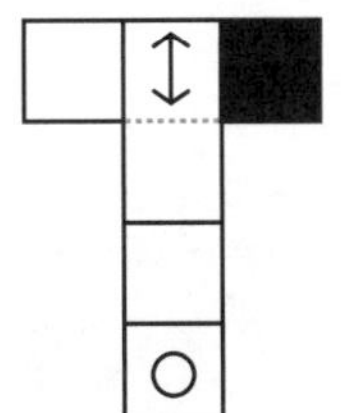

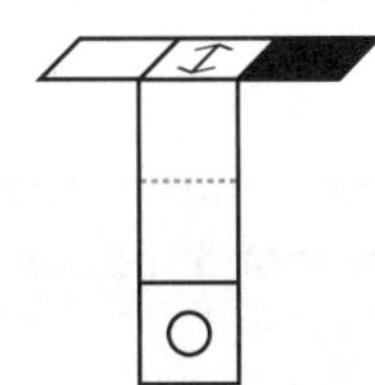

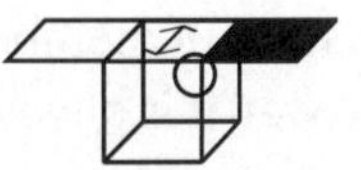

Start by folding the dotted joint between face 4 and face 1 so face 4 forms the top of the cube.

Next, fold face 5 along the dotted joint so it forms the bottom of the cube.

Now fold face 6 so it forms a seam with face 4.

Look at the direction of the arrow in relation to the circle on face 6.

Is it the same orientation as in the given cube? No, here the double-ended arrow is pointing towards the circle. In the cube, the arrow is parallel to the circle. Option **a** can be eliminated.

Moving on to option **b**:

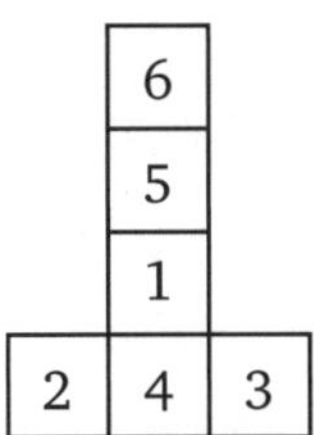

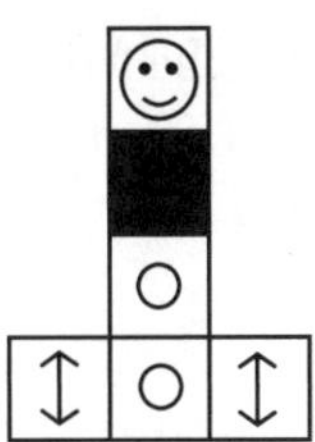

This net may look a bit confusing initially but it is still the T-shape; it has just been turned upside down. You can still examine it in the same way.

Look at the circle on face 4. You know that face 4 and face 5 will be opposite each other when the net is folded. In the cube, the circle is shown on an adjacent face to the black shaded square. Face 4 therefore cannot be the top of the cube.

This means you need to look at faces 2, 3, 1 and 5.

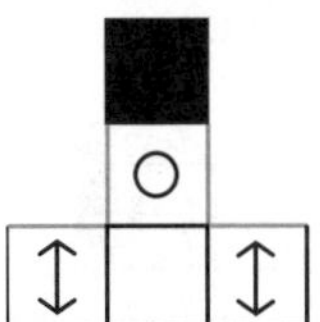

Think about how the borders of these faces will meet up to create the edges of the cube.

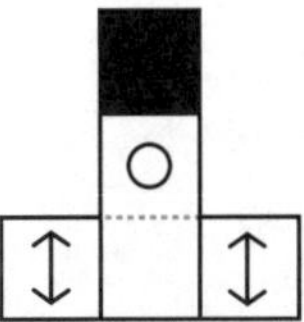

Fold face 4 along the dotted joint so it becomes the bottom of the cube.

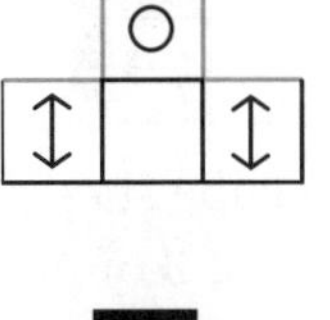

Now fold faces 2 and 3 upwards along the dotted joints.

What do you notice about the double-ended arrows? They have both changed direction and are now pointing towards the circle.

Option **b** can also be discounted at this point as the double-ended arrow should be parallel to the circle.

This leaves option **e** which, by this process of elimination, must be the answer. Remember, though, even if you think you have found the correct answer, it is always best to double-check.

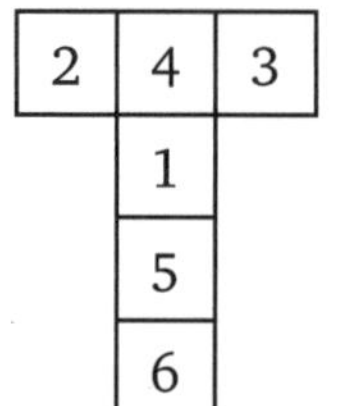

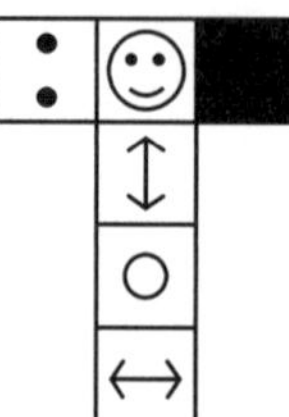

So, look at faces 3, 1, 5 and 6. How will the borders of these faces join to form edges of the cube? Follow the same step-by-step process as for the previous options.

Look at face 6. It has the same symbol as the front face of the given cube. So, to make the folding stages easier to visualise, imagine folding the net around face 6, keeping it as the front face.

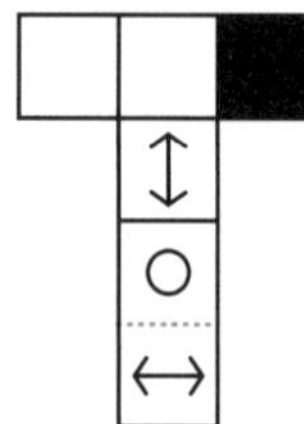

Fold face 5 along the dotted joint, making it the top of the cube.

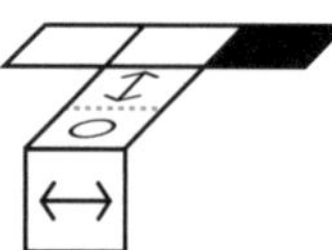

Then fold face 1 along the dotted joint to form the back of the cube.

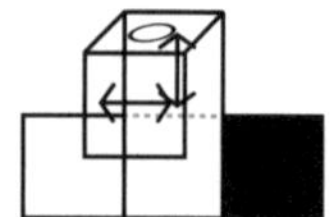

Next, fold face 4 along the dotted joint, making this face the bottom of the cube.

Can you see that this is the same as the given cube? If not, imagine folding face 3 upwards along the dotted joint to meet face 5.

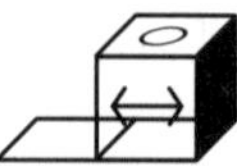

The given cube shows faces 6, 5 and 3 of option **e**. Option e is the correct answer.

REMEMBER!

When solving a net question, think of EOR:

Edges

Opposite

Rotation

Spatial awareness

This group of questions types tests your ability to manipulate a pattern and imagine what the transformed pattern will look like. You will need to apply logic and to work systematically to solve the questions. You will need to be able to:

- think systematically and make deductions about a transformed shape
- move between 2D and 3D representations of shape
- identify the features of a shape and imagine the features transformed.

The question types in this section have been presented together because they test similar logic and observational skills. However, they require different approaches. Some of the question types rely on the same sorts of skills used in the previous section, Rotating shapes, but they all share the need for spatial awareness.

For these questions you do not need to work out the link between a set of symbols. You are told what has happened to a given shape and you have to deduce which answer is the correct option.

There are five main types of spatial awareness questions. These are:

- Identify fold-and-punch patterns
- Recognise 2D views of 3D shapes
- Recognise 3D views of 2D shapes
- Recognise a 3D shape after rotation
- Identify shapes made from 3D building blocks

Now we'll work through this group of question types, looking at each one in turn.

Exam tips

Practise your sketching and listing techniques well ahead of the exam so you can work as quickly as possible on the day. To help you visualise a 3D shape in 2D, quickly sketch the top view, imagining it all squashed to the same height. You can then compare your quick sketch to the options available. For 'building block' questions, list the shapes that make up the answer options and check your list against the building blocks used.

9 *Identify fold-and-punch patterns*

This question type shows a piece of paper and how it is folded. This might be vertically, horizontally or diagonally. Dotted lines will show the folds, and arrows will show the direction of the folds. The final diagram shows the folded paper punched with one or more holes. In a standard format test, you will then be asked to draw the holes onto the unfolded image of the paper. In a multiple-choice test, you will be asked to choose the diagram that shows the holes in the correct position on the unfolded paper from several options. The two examples below are multiple-choice questions.

Look at this example.

A piece of paper is folded twice and then a hole is punched in the paper before it is unfolded. Which of these shapes shows the correct unfolded piece of paper? Circle the letter.

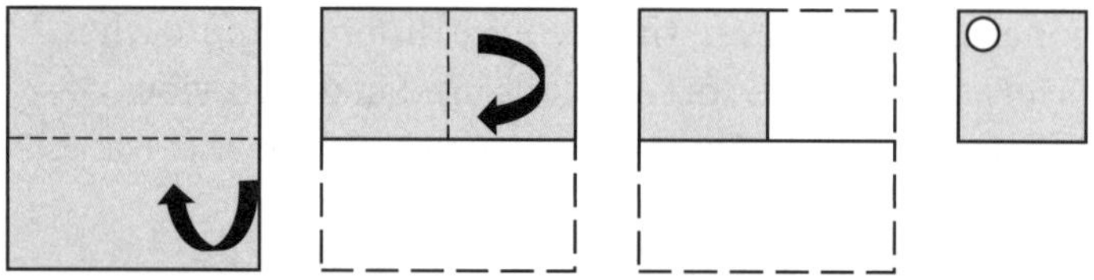

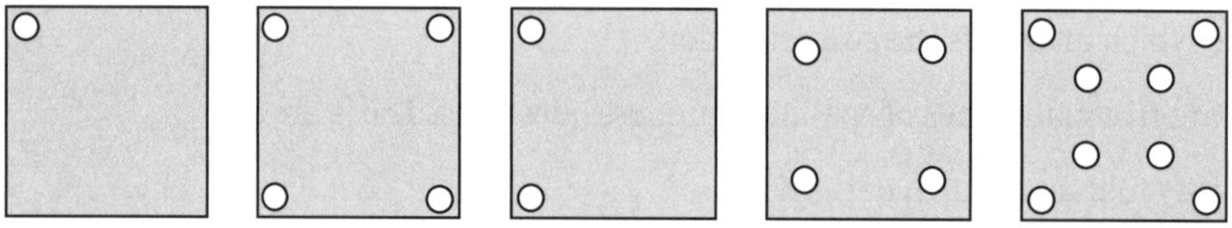

a b c d e

REMEMBER!

If the dashed lines to show the missing parts of the square have not been drawn, you can draw them in yourself. You can also work back through the sequence from right to left, drawing in each hole as you imagine unfolding the paper.

First, look at how many times the paper has been folded and how many holes have been punched into the paper. Here is a table showing how many holes you can expect to see depending on how many times the paper has been folded and how many holes have been punched in it.

		Number of holes punched into the folded paper				
		1 hole	2 holes	3 holes	4 holes	5 holes
Number of times the paper is folded	0 folds	1	2	3	4	5
	1 fold	2	4	6	8	10
	2 folds	4	8	12	16	20

You can see that the number of holes in the unfolded paper quickly multiplies. In the example above, the paper has two folds and one hole, so there will be four holes in the paper when it is unfolded. You can therefore reject options **a**, **c** and **e** straight away.

Now look at how close to the edge of the paper the hole is punched. In the example, the hole is punched within millimetres of the edge, so you can reject option **d**. The correct option must be **b** because it has exactly four holes, and the holes are positioned in the four corners.

Sometimes just the corner might be folded over, or the paper might be only folded halfway. To answer questions like this, you can think of the paper as two or more separate sections.

Look at this example.

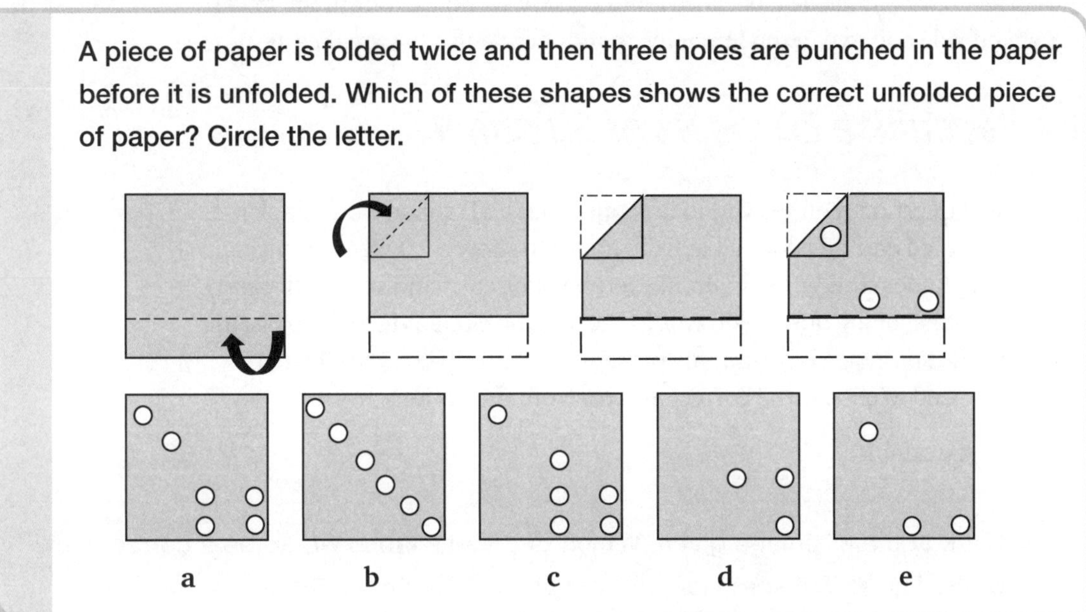

You can see that the paper has been folded a quarter of the way up, so the bottom outside edge will reach the halfway horizontal of the whole square. Next, the top left-hand corner has been folded on the diagonal. Three holes have then been punched. To work out what the paper will look like when it is unfolded, think about it in sections.

Think of the bottom half of the square as one section. It has one fold and two holes have been punched. So when the bottom half is unfolded, you will see four holes.

Think of the upper left quarter of the square as another section. It has one fold and one hole has been punched. So when the upper left corner is unfolded, you will see two holes.

That leaves the upper right quarter of the square. This has no folds and no holes.

REMEMBER!

Count the folds and holes to work out the total number of holes you will see when the paper is unfolded. Check how close the holes are to the edge of the paper.

You now know there will be six holes when the paper is unfolded, so you can reject options **d** and **e**.

Look carefully at the remaining three options, **a**, **b** and **c**.

The unfolded paper will have two holes in the top left-hand corner, so option **c** can be discounted.

The unfolded paper will have four holes in the bottom half, so option **b** can be discounted.

The correct option must be **a** because it has exactly six holes: four in the lower right-hand side and two in the upper left-hand section in a diagonal pattern.

10 Recognise 2D views of 3D shapes

This type of question requires you to imagine what a 3D shape would look like if it were rotated and then looked at from above to show a 2D view. If you can imagine a cylinder standing upright like a tube of biscuits and you then stand above the tube looking down, you would see just the circular top of the biscuit tube. This question type is commonly presented in multiple-choice format, where you need to choose the correct answer from the options given.

Look at this example.

Look at the 3D image given. Which of these shapes would be a correct view of the image if it were viewed from above? Circle the letter.

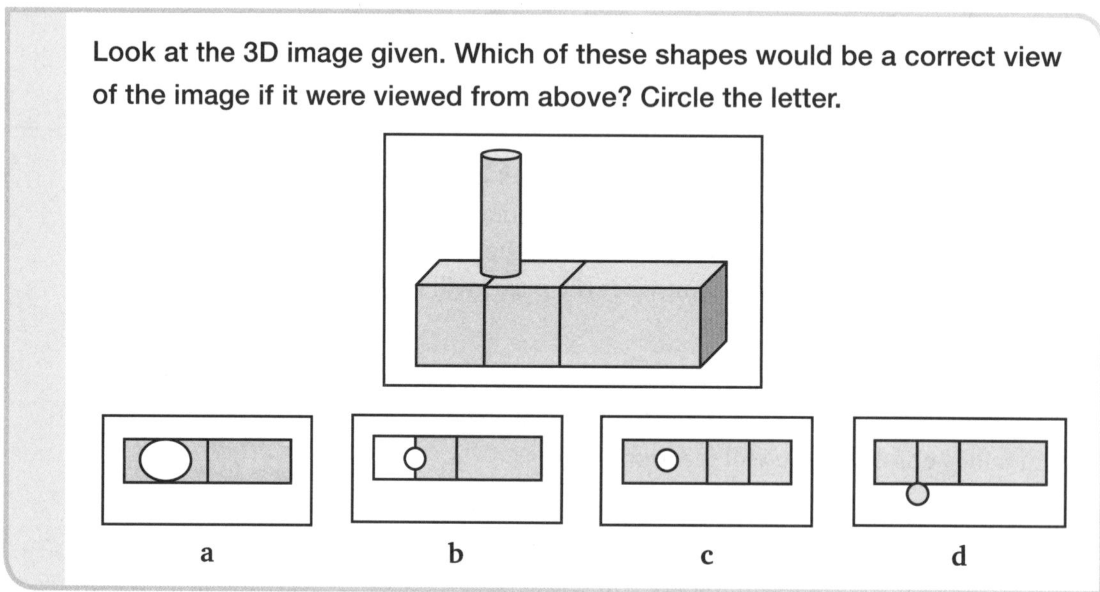

First, imagine looking at the 3D shape from above, and count how many shapes you would be able to see. For this shape, you would be able to see four shapes: one rectangle, two squares and one circle. Then look at the four answer options. Can you see all four shapes in each option?

In option **a** you cannot clearly see the two squares because the circle is covering the joint between them. In the 3D image, there is a space around the cylinder and you can clearly see the two cubes. You can therefore reject option **a**.

Next, look at how the shapes are placed on top of each other. Are the shapes on top, to the side, to the back? In the 3D image, the cylinder is on top of the other shapes. Look at the remaining three answer options. In option **d**, the cylinder is at the side of the cubes. You can therefore reject option **d**.

Now look at the joins between the cuboid and cubes. In the 3D image, the two cubes are on the left of the cuboid, with the cylinder on top of the cubes. In option **c**, the cylinder is on the left but it is on top of the cuboid. You can therefore reject option **c**.

The correct option must be **b**. It has the two cubes on the left of the cuboid, with the cylinder on top of the cubes.

11 Recognise 3D views of 2D shapes

This type of question requires you to imagine what a 2D shape would look like if it were in 3D. If you can imagine standing on a castle or tall building and looking directly down, the ground below appears to be in 2D even though you know this isn't really the case. This question type is commonly presented in multiple-choice format, where you need to choose the correct answer from the options given.

Look at this example.

Look at the 2D image given. Which of these shapes would be a correct view of the image if it were viewed in 3D format? Circle the letter.

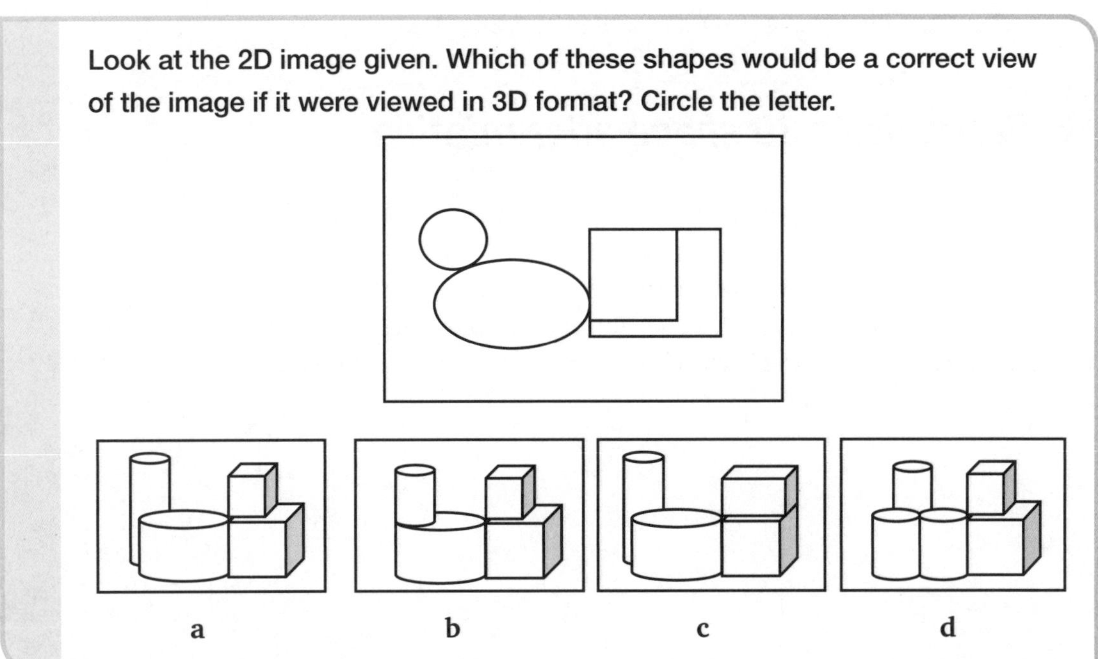

You can approach this type of question in a similar way to the previous question type. Imagine looking at the 3D shapes from above, and work out which one matches the 2D image given.

REMEMBER!

When comparing 2D and 3D views of a combination of shapes, count the shapes, and also think about how the shapes are positioned and about any spaces between and around them.

Begin by counting how many shapes you can see from above. In this example there are four shapes: a circle, an oval, a square and a rectangle. Then look at the four answer options and imagine looking at them from above. Would you be able to see all four shapes in each option? In option **d** you would see three circles or ovals from above. You can therefore reject option **d**.

Next, look at how the shapes are placed in relation to each other. Are the shapes on top, to the side, to the back? In the 2D image, the circle is behind the oval. Imagine looking at the remaining three answer options from above. If you looked at option **b** from above, you would see the circle inside the oval. You can therefore reject option **b**.

Now look at how much space there is between and around the shapes. From the 2D image, you can see that the cube is on top of the cuboid and there is a space between the right-hand edge of the cube and the right-hand edge of the cuboid, as well as a smaller space at the front. In option **c**, there is a space at the front but the shape on top is a cuboid the same width as the bottom one. You can therefore reject option **c**.

The correct option must be **a** because it has one smaller cube on top of a larger cuboid and one circular cylinder behind an oval cylinder.

12 *Recognise a 3D shape after rotation*

This type of question tests your ability to look at a shape and imagine how it would look if it were rotated. You need to be able to think logically and to manipulate a shape by recognising common features and how they would look in a different perspective. This question is commonly presented as a multiple-choice question where you choose the correct answer from the options given.

Look at this example.

The 3D images below have been rotated. Which of these shapes matches the original shape? Circle the letter.

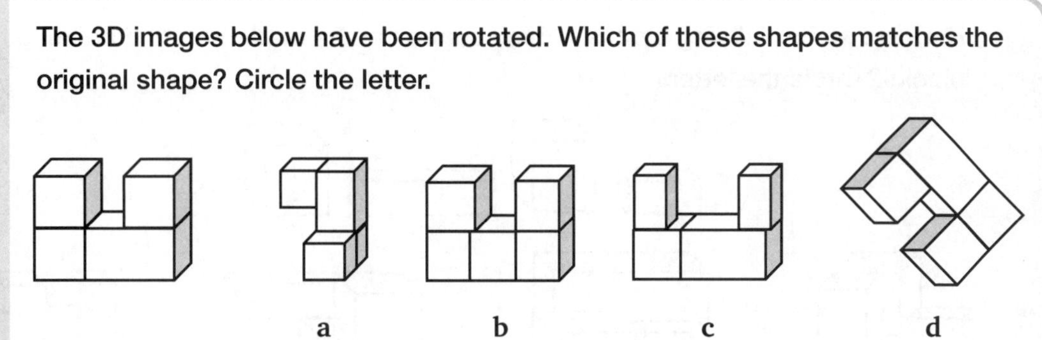

To find the correct rotation, first familiarise yourself with the original shape.

- How many blocks have been used to make the shape?
- Is part of any of the blocks obscured? For example, you might be looking at the end of a cuboid, and its full length might be hidden.
- Is there anything special about the outline? Which parts of the image are shorter or longer? Are there any gaps?

First, work out how many blocks have been used to form the shape. In the example above you can see three cubes and one cuboid. You can immediately reject option **b** because it has five cubes and no cuboid. You can also reject option **c** because it has one cube and three cuboids (one large and two smaller ones).

Next look at the unique feature of the shape above. It is a 'U' shape. You can therefore reject option **a** because it is a different shape.

The correct option must be **d**. It shows the shape rotated anticlockwise by 135°.

REMEMBER!

When you first look at a shape, see its unique pattern. Does it look like a letter? Does it remind you of an object? Once you can think of this unique pattern, it is easier to picture it rotated. Check whether each option has the same unique pattern – if not, that option can be quickly rejected.

13 *Identify shapes made from 3D building blocks*

This type of question tests your ability to understand how shapes are constructed and how they can be manipulated. You will need to work systematically and logically to work out which shapes could be made from the given blocks.

Look at this example.

Here are some building blocks. Which shape can be made from the building blocks? Circle the letter.

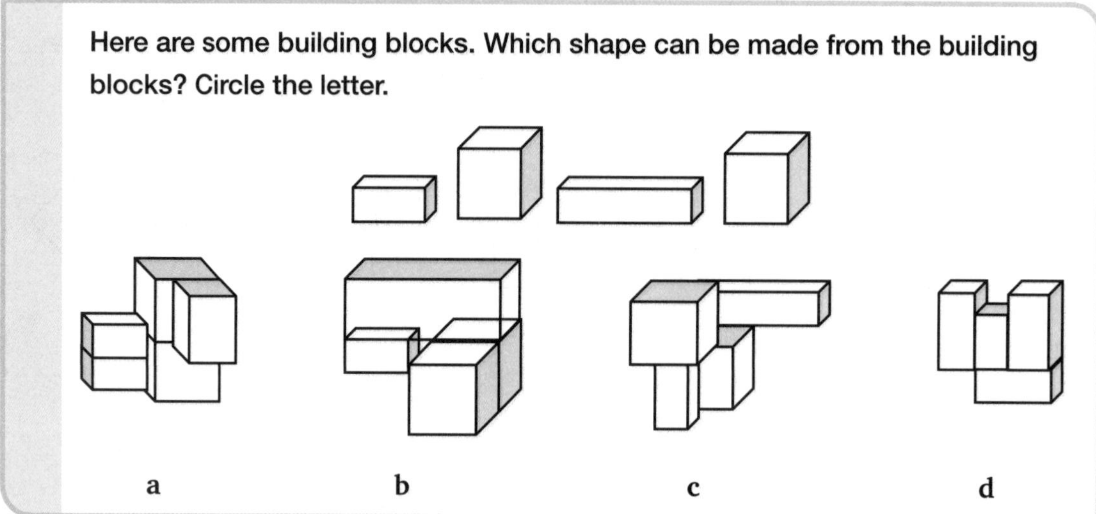

To find the correct answer option, look carefully at the blocks in each shape and see if they match the given blocks.

First, count the number of blocks given and see which shapes have the correct number of blocks. In this example, there are four blocks. You can therefore reject option **a** straight away because it is made of five blocks.

Next, check whether any of the shapes are the same. In this example, there are two identical cubes, and two different cuboids. Now look at the remaining three options. You can reject option **d** because it has three cuboids of the same size, and no cubes.

Now look at the remaining two options and check whether the blocks used are the same size, shape and length of the blocks given. In this example, the two cuboids are the same width and depth, although one is longer than the other. In option **b**, the larger cuboid, which is on the top, is too wide and too deep. You can therefore reject option **b**.

The correct option must be c. It is made from two identical cubes and two cuboids of the same width and depth, but different lengths.

REMEMBER!

If it is easier, you can number the building blocks and then look at each option to see if it contains each block in turn. Begin by asking yourself 'Does option **a** contain a block the same shape and size as block 1?' If it does, look for block 2. If it doesn't, you can reject option **a** and move on to option **b**.

Coded shapes and logic

This group of questions tests your understanding of shape but you also need to apply your logic skills. To solve these questions you need the ability to:

- think systematically and make deductions about a set of symbols
- find and apply a given rule
- identify common features
- see shapes within shapes.

These question types have been sorted into the same group as they test similar logic and observation skills. However, they require different approaches. For the first question type in this group, it is useful to look again at the spider diagram that was introduced in the earlier sections, Identifying shapes and Missing shapes:

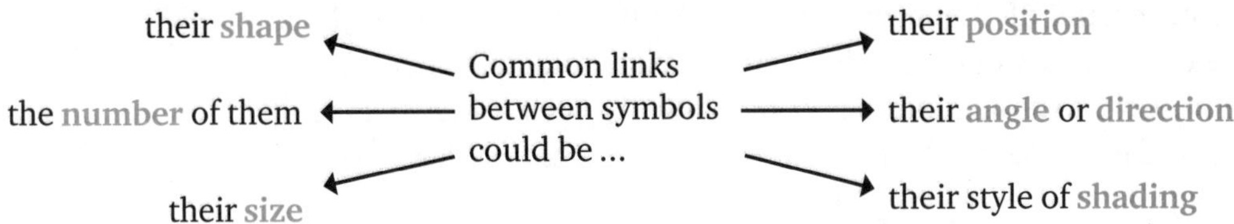

You know now that links betw7

n a series of symbols or patterns can be based on one or more of these features. These elements will also help you to identify the rules behind sets of coded symbols.

There are two main sets of coded shapes and logic questions. These are:

- Code and decode shapes
- Apply shape logic

As questions based on shape logic do not require you to think about these links, start by looking at coded shapes.

14 *Code and decode shapes*

These questions are often referred to as codes or coded sequences. You may be familiar with this type of question from verbal reasoning papers. In both verbal and non-verbal reasoning, questions involving codes test your logic and deduction skills as well as your ability to work out and follow sequences and patterns. The difference with non-verbal reasoning codes is that you have to understand how visual features relate to letter codes, rather than how words relate to them.

Usually a question will present a series of patterns or symbols in a line, with each symbol except one having a unique code that is made up of two letters. You must then use your analysis skills to work out the rule behind the code and apply it correctly to find the missing code for the unlabelled symbol.

Here is a straightforward example.

Which code matches the shape or pattern given at the end of the line? Circle the letter.

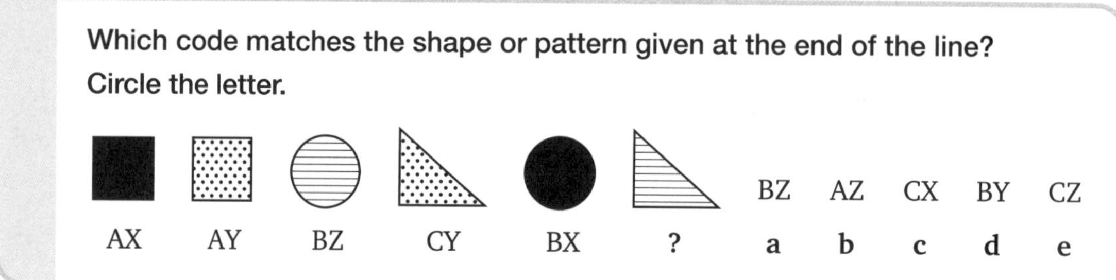

All codes stand for, or represent, something else. In the case of non-verbal reasoning, each letter of a code will represent a different feature or element of the given series of symbols. The first letter in each code will always stand for the same feature throughout the series. Similarly, the next letter of each code will stand for a second element throughout the whole series.

You need to find a connection between two or more symbols that share part of the code. The most effective way to do this is to approach the question systematically.

Start by looking at each coded symbol.

Are there any symbols that share their first code letter? Yes.

These two symbols must therefore have a common feature.

These are both squares.

It looks like the first letter of this code relates to the **shape** of a symbol. To be sure that you have found the correct link for the first letter, check if any more symbols share the same first code letter.

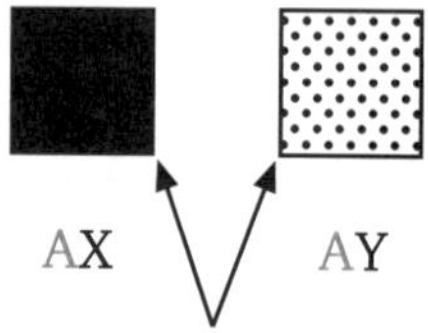

Exam tips

These questions can take up a lot of time in an exam. It is worth putting in additional practice so that you can answer them as quickly as possible. Remember to look straight away at shared first letter codes and decide what common element they share. Follow this with the shared second letter codes to decide what common element they share.

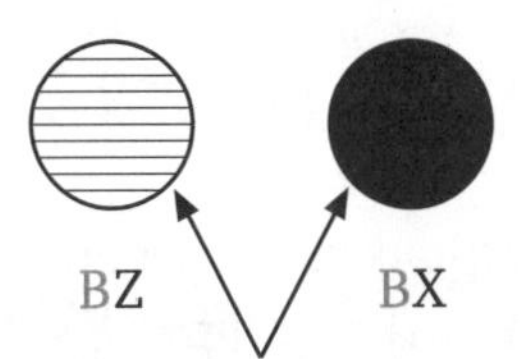

The codes for these two symbols also start with the same letter.

They are both circles.

This confirms that the first letter of the code reflects the shape of a symbol.

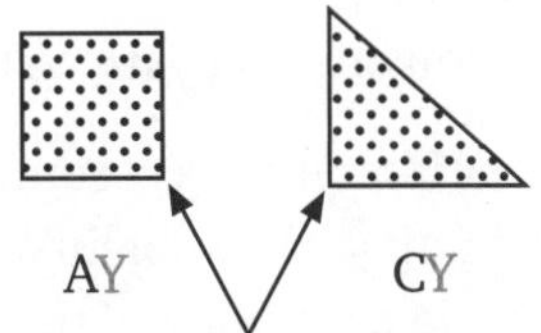

Now think about the second code letters.

Are there any symbols that share their second letter? Yes.

What do these symbols have in common?

They are both shaded with dots.

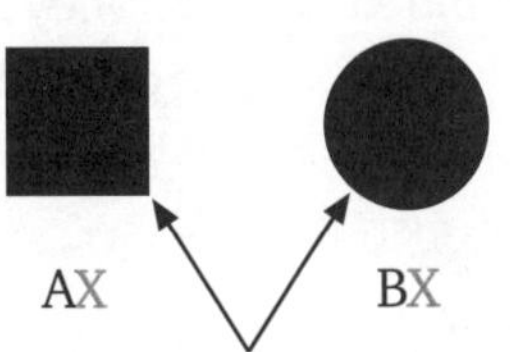

It looks like the second letter of this code relates to the **shading** of a symbol. Again, to be sure that you have found the correct link, check with another pair of symbols.

The codes for these two symbols also have the same second letter.

They are both shaded black.

This confirms that the second letter of the code reflects the shading of a symbol.

Now that you have worked out the rules behind the code, you can find the missing code for the unlabelled symbol.

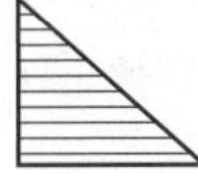

Think about what the symbol is: **a right-angled triangle with horizontally-striped shading**.

Now look for the symbols that share the same shape and shading.

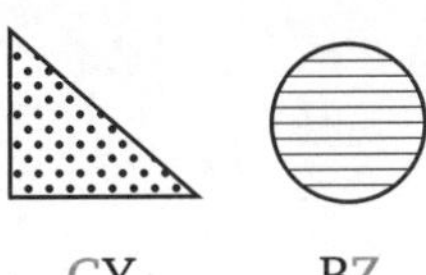

The code for the unlabelled symbol must be CZ, option **e**.

REMEMBER!

If you cannot find the link immediately, try describing what you can see as this can help you focus on common elements.

REMEMBER!

Sometimes a code question will be presented in a different format (in a grid for example) or the code will have been formed using more than two digits and a combination of letters and numbers. If you are given a set of questions in a different format, don't panic! You can still use the same logical thought processes to find the missing code.

REMEMBER!

As for many question types, make sure you work from left to right to ensure you don't overlook any elements.

15 Apply shape logic

The questions in this set are often called combined shapes. Usually a question in this group will show you two shapes and ask you to select the shape or pattern that is made when they are combined. In a similar way to hidden shapes questions, you therefore need to use your powers of observation and analysis to spot individual shapes within given patterns.

This question type may seem very straightforward, as questions do not rely on you finding common links between a group of symbols. Although the size or style of shading of the individual shapes will not change when they are combined, they may be rotated and appear at a different angle within the combined pattern. They may also overlap each other, which can make the individual shapes difficult to identify. As with all non-verbal reasoning questions, make sure you look at all aspects carefully to avoid making careless mistakes.

Some combined shapes questions will be easier to work out than others. Don't worry if you cannot see an answer straight away. If you approach these questions methodically, you will be able to find the answer. Look at this example that may appear quite difficult at first glance.

Which shape or pattern is made when the first two shapes or patterns are put together? Circle the letter.

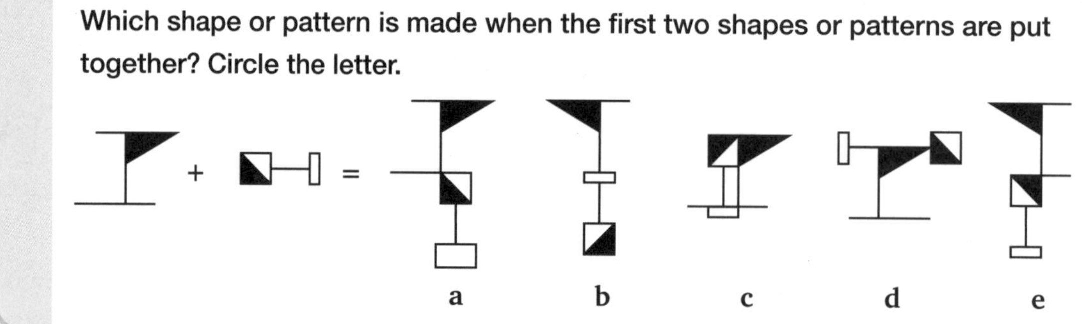

An effective way to tackle these questions is to look for each separate symbol in turn. Remember, the symbols may have been rotated when being combined, so they may not appear exactly as they do when separated.

So, in this example you could start by looking at the first symbol.

Compare the given symbol with the version included in each option. Which options contain an accurate representation of the symbol?

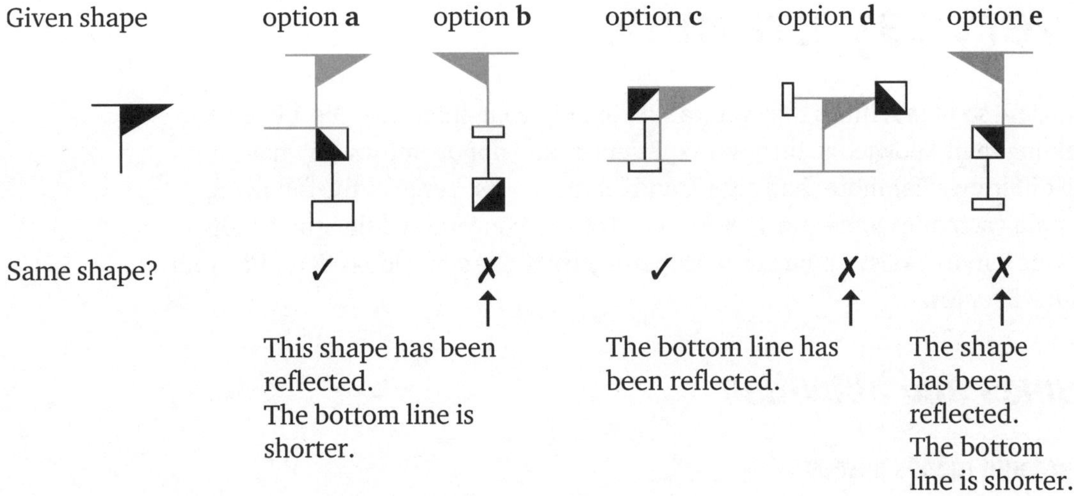

Examining the first symbol in each of the options has shown that options **b**, **d** and **e** cannot be the correct answer. These can therefore be eliminated.

Now compare the versions of the second symbol in options **a** and **c**. Which one shows an exact copy?

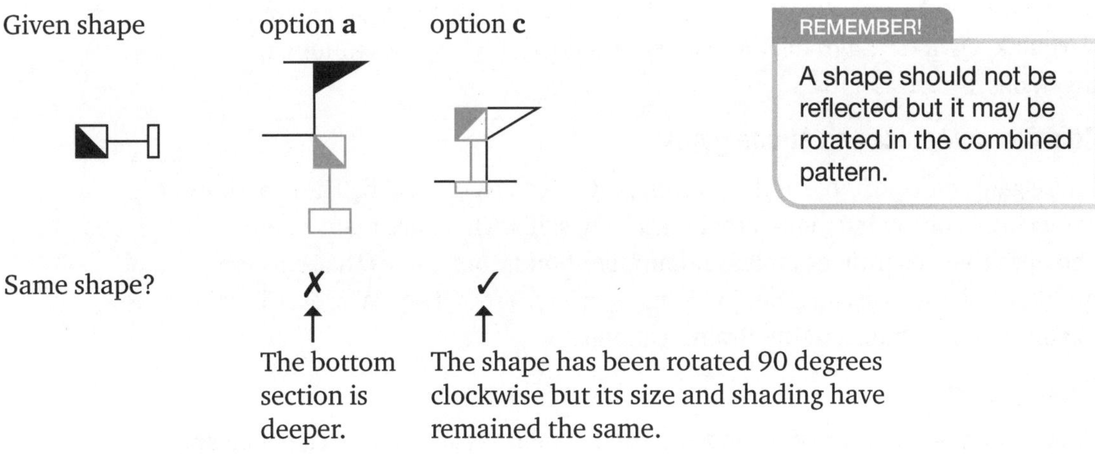

REMEMBER!

A shape should not be reflected but it may be rotated in the combined pattern.

Option **c** must therefore be the correct answer.

Everyday practice

There are so many things that you can do to help your child with the 11+. Building their knowledge through experiences and opportunities can make a real difference, far more than sitting and learning lists. Some of the following everyday activities underpin 11+ knowledge and concepts, while others help to provide a more holistic education. Hopefully there are some ideas here that your child will enjoy.

Games and activities

Board and pieces games

These are games that use either a board or pieces. They can extend skills in numeracy, data, shape, space, strategic thinking, logic and problem solving, and they do so in a fun way. Specialised games can be found on teacher resource websites, but many games can be readily accessed in high street and online shops. Some libraries allow you to borrow games, and charity shops can be great places to buy board games. Here are some examples of games that reinforce skills, and are also fun to play: 221B Baker Street, Jenga, Battleship, Sequence, Connect 4, Simon Air, Azul, chess, Rummikub, Disney Villainous, Rapidough, Pictionary, Kerplunk, Qwirkle, Sagrada, dominoes, Othello, draughts, backgammon, Ingenious, Shaperise, Risk.

Console, computer and phone games

These games are portable and are often played by just one child. They can both extend and consolidate non-verbal reasoning skills. There are many games and apps that cover times tables and number bonds, but games that develop problem-solving skills include The Sims, SimCity, Tetris, Lego Worlds, Cities Skylines, Buzz! Brain and Big Brain Academy.

Paper games

These games are quick to play and are also portable – you just need a pencil and some paper. You can vary the games according to the age and ability of your child. For example, battleships with a younger child could have only vertical and horizontal ships, and only a small area of sea. Paper games that extend non-verbal reasoning skills include lines and squares, tic-tac-toe and battleships.

Active games

If you have a sandpit or paddling pool, activities that include hands-on components can consolidate problem solving skills, especially if you make the task specific. For example, challenge your child to use paper to build a bridge that crosses an area of water and can hold the weight of a toy car. How about building a sand structure that reaches 50 cm tall, or creating a water course through dams and bridges?

Other hands-on activities

These are games or activities that one child can do by themselves. The activities can take as much time as the child wants to spend on them. Such activities strengthen skills in strategic thinking, problem solving and shape/space awareness. Here are some examples of hands-on activities that help to strengthen key non-verbal reasoning skills:

- Construction games or toys that have a diagram with a step-by-step guide for children to follow, or that allow them to create their own original constructs; for example, Lego, K'nex, Meccano or Airfix models.
- Jigsaw puzzles – the number of pieces and the subject matter can be varied to suit the ability and interests of the child.
- 'Where's Wally?', spot the difference or similar puzzle games.
- Origami, paper aeroplane kits or other modelling.
- Rubik's cube – challenge your child to work as quickly as possible to solve it.
- Mosaics and bead crafts that rely on pattern, repetition and order.
- Weaving, plaiting friendship bands and other crafts that require following a pattern strengthen skills in sequences, shape, colour and pattern awareness.

Top ten everyday activities

Everyday activities can make a surprising difference to how your child thinks and develops non-verbal logic. For example, using a compass helps to develop a sense of direction and rotation, while understanding sequences and patterns helps to develop a sense of order and repetition. These are all valuable skills that will support formal non-verbal reasoning lessons.

1 Improve your child's analysis and visual connection skills by setting them a puzzle using everyday items. For example, place a 10 pence piece and 10 counters on a table. Then put a 2 pence piece down and place a range of different items in groups on the other side of the table, such as two sweets, four crayons, six pencils, five cups and a five pence piece. Explain that there is a link between the 10 pence piece and the 10 counters and they need to find that link and use it to place an item or items next to the 2 pence piece. If a 10 pence piece is linked to 10 counters, then the 2 pence piece should be linked to two items. Timing these puzzles will make the game more challenging and exciting. This game can be as easy or difficult as you want.

2 Give your child a fun sequence to create at meal times. For example, ask your child to make a sequence of five peas and three pieces of sweetcorn, followed by five pieces of sweetcorn and three peas, and continue until they run out of peas or sweetcorn. Then they can eat their vegetable sequence!

3 If your child struggles with direction, give them a compass (available cheaply online) when you are in the car and ask them to make a note of the directions the car travels in. Once your child feels more confident with direction, ask them to find an alternative way home using the compass.

4 Play the robot game. Your child is a robot and can only move in the pattern that you give them. Say, for example, "Forward three steps, then turn 90° clockwise. Now forward six steps, then turn 90° clockwise." This is a game that children like to play together. Added fun can be created by awarding marks for the best moving robot.

5 If your child struggles with rotation, cut out some shapes from a piece of paper that is coloured on one side. Work with triangles, circles,

squares and rectangles – perhaps five of each shape. Rotate the shapes and see how they look when they are flipped over. Ask your child to use the shapes to make a robot or alien and then transform the same pieces to make a row of flowers or another pattern.

6 When you have a shopping trolley at the supermarket, ask your child to put the items in the trolley with as few gaps between each item as possible. Encourage them to rotate the shapes of tins, boxes and jars to fit in as many as possible. This is a great way of getting them to develop spatial awareness and to practise problem-solving. Some children enjoy ordering items and making order out of chaos, but if your child does not have tidy pencil cases and drawers, even getting them to put 'like with like' can help. Encourage them to organise crayons in one tub all facing the same way or to place books by colour or size order on shelves. These activities will reinforce why objects are the same or different, and they can build skills that will help your child when they have to find the odd shape out or shapes that are related in some way.

7 Create a domino run – see how many exciting shapes your child can make before pushing over the first domino. Video the run so you can re-watch it and discuss what worked best and whether there were any problems that could be solved next time.

8 Create a mini fairy garden in a plant pot using feathers, grass, kitchen foil, small plants and plastic toys as decorations. Once complete, ask your child to draw their fairy-garden. This ability to draw a 3D space in 2D is a key skill in non-verbal reasoning.

9 Try communicating with your child by sending them an email or text made totally from emojis, symbols and numbers. Signs that show happy, sad or joking are easy enough, but a message that suggests "your breakfast is ready and if you are not down here within 5 minutes I shall be annoyed with you" will prove more challenging.

10 If you have fresh snow, make the most of it by giving your child a pattern to follow. For example, ask them to "Left-leg hop, left-leg hop, jump, right-leg hop, right-leg hop, jump" and then look at the pattern they have made. Encourage them to follow a pattern to make the outlines of a circle or a rectangle.

Notes

Great Clarendon Street, Oxford, OX2 6DP, United Kingdom

Oxford University Press is a department of the University of Oxford. It furthers the University's objective of excellence in research, scholarship, and education by publishing worldwide. Oxford is a registered trade mark of Oxford University Press in the UK and in certain other countries

First published in 2020

British Library Cataloguing in Publication Data
Data available

978-0-19-277618-1

10 9 8 7 6 5 4 3

Paper used in the production of this book is a natural, recyclable product made from wood grown in sustainable forests. The manufacturing process conforms to the environmental regulations of the country of origin.

Printed in Poland by Opolgraf SA

Acknowledgements

The Publishers would like to thank Michellejoy Hughes for her contribution to this edition.

Cover illustrations by Lo Cole